Membership Records *of* Seventh Day Baptist Churches *in* Western New York *and* Northwestern Pennsylvania

1800-1900

Ilou M. Sanford

HERITAGE BOOKS
2008

HERITAGE BOOKS
AN IMPRINT OF HERITAGE BOOKS, INC.

Books, CDs, and more—Worldwide

For our listing of thousands of titles see our website
at
www.HeritageBooks.com

Published 2008 by
HERITAGE BOOKS, INC.
Publishing Division
100 Railroad Ave. #104
Westminster, Maryland 21157

Copyright © 1996 Ilou M. Sanford

Other books by the author:
First Alfred Seventh Day Baptist Church Membership Records, Alfred, New York
Membership Records of Seventh Baptists of Central New York State, 1797-1940s
Newport Seventh Day Baptist Trilogy
Ilou M. Sanford and Don A. Sanford

All rights reserved. No part of this book may be reproduced or transmitted in any form or by any means, electronic or mechanical, including photocopying, recording or by any information storage and retrieval system without written permission from the author, except for the inclusion of brief quotations in a review.

International Standard Book Numbers
Paperbound: 978-0-7884-0462-7
Clothbound: 978-0-7884-7176-6

FOREWORD

Membership Records of Seventh Day Baptist Churches in Western New York and Northwestern Pennsylvania - 1800 - 1900 - Ilou M. Sanford. From the church record collection at the Seventh Day Baptist Historical Society Archives housed at Janesville, WI comes a third compilation from original records of forty churches containing over 2500 admissions with a sprinkling of other facts. Since Seventh Day Baptists were often among the first wave of settlers, this book is a must for people tracking early Rhode Island, Eastern New York and New Jersey families. Many non-traditional SDB families were caught up in the evangelistic fervor of the era and joined local churches. Some belonged for brief periods of time; others joined in the western migration into Wisconsin, Iowa and Nebraska.

HISTORICAL BACKGROUND

The churches included in this compilation of Seventh Day Baptist church records for the period of this study were known as the Western Association of Seventh Day Baptist Churches. In 1968 the name was changed to the Allegheny Association. It comprised the land west of what was called a Pre-emption Line drawn from Sodus Bay on Lake Ontario (north of Seneca Lake) to the Pennsylvania line. Both Massachusetts and New York claimed this land prior to the Revolutionary War. In 1786 a compromise was reached whereby Massachusetts was granted all of the land west of that line for disposal purposes only, while New York was given sovereignty over it. Massachusetts was thus only interested in the money derived from the initial sale and turned to quick sales to large land speculators to pay some of its huge war debts. These land companies began to mark trails into the area, but it was only after the War of 1812 and the removal of Indian threats through resettlement and treaty that the territory was settled to any extent. Many of the early settlers were veterans or sons of veterans of the Revolutionary War or the War of 1812.

Seventh Day Baptist settlers began filtering into this territory from churches in Rhode Island, Rensselaer and Madison Counties in eastern and central New York State. The initial settlement was made in the Alfred area of eastern Allegany County, (the county was spelled Allegany while the river and its basin were spelled Allegheny). Families fanned out from Alfred into surrounding territories to the west and south, including settlements in northern Pennsylvania. A smaller migration came directly from Rhode Island and settled on one of the tributaries of the Allegheny River at Little Genesee where a cemetery still carries the name Little Rhode Island.

The proliferation of churches in this area can be attributed to two basic factors: geography and evangelism. In the highlands of the Appalachian region, the shortest distance between two points is not a straight line. Two major divides separated Allegany County in New York and Potter County in Pennsylvania with the water in the eastern portions flowing into the Susquehanna River to Chesapeake Bay; that in the central portion was drained by the Genesee River flowing north into Lake Ontario and the St. Lawrence River; while the western portion was a part of the Allegheny, Ohio and Mississippi River basin emptying into the Gulf of Mexico. Many of the communities were isolated and travel was difficult, particularly in the winter and spring months.

A second reason for the many scattered churches or branches may be attributed to the influence of Alfred University. Following the Civil War, an evangelistic fervor hit the students and the faculty at Alfred. Teams of students went out on week-ends and conducted revival services in many of the small settlements in the area. In 1871 the theological department of the college was granted a charter as a graduate seminary and a number of its students, often with the assistance of one of the professors, gave pastoral service as time permitted. Churches were sometimes established, but without sustained leadership, most did not last long. Furthermore, without the family ties and heritage which characterized those churches that were established by migrations from other Seventh Day Baptist churches, the sense of denominational loyalty was lacking and many converts turned to other churches.

Some of the churches in Pennsylvania were also hampered by the strict Sunday Blue laws of 1794 which prohibited work on Sunday. For Sabbathkeeping churches, this had the effect of restricting their work week to five days and produced an economic problem. Even farmers were at times arrested for work on Sunday. As the many small farms dwindled many of the people depended on other forms of employment which led to the demise of these rural oriented communities and their institutions.

Rev. Don A. Sanford, Historian
Seventh Day Baptist Historical Society
Janesville, Wisconsin

Membership Records
of Seventh Day Baptist Churches
in Western New York and Northwestern Pennsylvania
1800- 1900

List of Abbreviations

ad	----	admitted
c	----	about
d	----	died
dec	----	deceased
dis	----	dismissed
d/o	----	daughter of
dp	----	dropped
ex	----	excluded
excom	----	excommunicated
fr	----	from
gc/o	----	grandchild of
gd/o	----	granddaughter of
gd/s	----	grandson of
nr	----	non-resident
prob	----	probably
rem	----	removed
rest	----	restored
rj	----	rejected
s/o	----	son of
w/o	----	wife of
wid/o	----	widow of

CRR.???? ----- SDB Historical So. accession number for church records

Membership Records of Seventh Day Baptist Churches in Western New York and Northwestern Pennsylvania 1800-1900

TABLE OF CONTENTS

Foreword
Historical Background
Abbreviations

I. Eastern Allegany and Steuben Counties New York
Second Alfred	1
Hartsville	14
Andover	18
Independence	22
Troupsburg	27
Hornellsville	28

II. Central Allegany County
Angelica	29
Amity	30
Scio	31
Wellsville	32
Scio Branch	34
Stannard's Corners	34
Friendship (Nile)	35
Richburg	45

III. The Genesees
First Genesee (Little Genesee)	53
Second Genesee (Portville)	62
Third Genesee (West Genesee)	63
Little Rhode Island Cemetery	68

IV. The Buffalo Area Churches

- Clarence 72
- Pendleton 75
- Darien-Cowlesville 76
- Wilson 77
- Clarence and Pendleton 78
- Persia 79

V. Northwestern Pennsylvania

- First Hebron (Crandall Hill) 81
- Ulysses 88
- Allegheny River (Roulette) 88
- Hebron Center 89
- Shinglehouse 90
- Bells Run 91
- Honeoye Branch 91
- Fox 92
- Shiloh 93
- Hayfield 94
- Cussewago 94
- Hickernell 94

Appendix

- Civil War Soldiers 95
- List of Ministers and Missionaries 99
- Timeline 100
- Maps 101
- Index 103

I. SEVENTH DAY BAPTIST CHURCHES IN EASTERN ALLEGANY AND STEUBEN COUNTIES
(First Alfred listed in separate book)

Second Alfred 1831-
Allegany Co. NY
1st located at Goose Pasture or Pleasant Valley:
next met in the village called Bakers Bridge, now called Alfred Station

Constituent Members

Dea. Amos Burdick Jr
Jesse Saunders - dis
Nathan Lanphear - ordained deacon Aug 23'32
Edward Green
Jesse S. Whitford - d 1848
Stephen R. Smith - ordained deacon Aug 23'32, dis

p. 2
Robert Bloomer - d
Elisha Potter
Oliver H. P. Hull - dis
Nathan V. Hull - dis
Hezekiah Bentley - ex

Jonathan Lanphear - d WI
Daniel Maxson - dis
Benjamin Green - rj
Paris Green
Silas Benjamin - d 1836

Thomas Benjamin - d
Oliver Coon
Jeremiah Davis
David B. Satterlee
Roumanzo Brooks - rj

Members

Esther Saunders - dis
Susan Maxson - dis
Polly Beebe - ex '33
Huldah Green - d

p. 3
Syntha Wright - dis
Hannah Smith - d Feb'39
Diadamia Benjamin
Fanny Potter - dis
Hannah Hull
Lydia Burdick
Lydia M. Burdick - m Palmiter, ex
Mercy Leskin - d 1850
Sally Head - dis
Sylvia Bentley - dis
Eunice Franklin - dis

Elizabeth Burdick
Syntha Lanphear
Sally Green - dis
Elizabeth A. Green - d

Mary Green - d Jun'32
Olive Whitford - gone '31
Hannah Burdick - d '51
Hariot Coon - d
Patty Hull - dis '37
Caty Burdick
Tacy Burdick - m Shaw
Mercy Davis - dis
Eunice H. Whitford
Fanny Young - d Apr'41
Polly Green

Members added in 1831 & 1832

p. 4
Theodaty Bliven - bp, dis
Clark Potter Jr - dis '37
Ray Green - licentiate, ordained elder Aug 23'32
Stephen Maxson - dis
Jonathan B. Potter - bp, ex
Jesse Whitford - bp, d 1851
Jonathan Lanphear 2nd - bp
Varnum Hull - bp, dis
John Hill - bp, rj '37

Henry Withy - ex
Solomon Head
Clark Green
Moses B. Cheesbrough - bap, rj
John Benjamin - bp, d 1838
Franklin Burdick - bp
Silas Lanphear - bp, d '48
Ichabod Babcock - bp
Clarke Green

p. 5
Elihu Babcock - bp, d Sep '35
Jason Beebe - bp
Asa Green - bp
Seth Beebe - ex
Edward Hawkl - bp, gone (crossed out)
Joshua Green - bp, gone
Jesse Babcock - dis
Jeremiah Green - rj
Elijah Lewis
Thomas Green - bp, dis

p. 7
Clarissa Withy - ex '35
Charlotte Withy - ex '34, m Miner
Sarah Beebe - d '37
Mary Potter - bp, d Jun'32
Betsey Potter - bp, dis '37
Sinthy Benjamin - bp, dis '37
Ruth Baker - bp, dis
Prudence Babcock bp, dis
Lydia Shaw - bp, m Lewis, ex
Selah Babcock - bp
Martha Lanphear - bp, dis

p. 8
Susannah Green Lanphear - bp
Avildy Babcock - bp, m Hemplill
Angelina Green - bp, m, dis
Esther *Beely Lanphear - bp, m
Eunice Lanphear - d '37
Sally Lewis
Catherine Burdick - bp, m, d Aug 16'42
Lois Green - bp, m Claer, d '54
Huldah Green Hull - bp
Anna Lewis Marrow - bp, m

Edward Green 3rd - bp
Leonard Potter - bp, ex
Ransolaer Green - bp, dis
Seth Beebe Jr - ex '33
Darias Saterlee
Charles Smith - bp
Russel Lewis - bp, d Jul'36
Amos Ellis - dis '37
George S. Coon
George B. Popple - bp, excom

Lydia A. Withy - ex '35
Thalla Hull - dis
Prudence Cheesbrough - dis
Caty Hill - bp, dis
Jane Head - bp, m, dis
Anna Green - bp, m Place
Lucy Green - bp, dis
Mary Davis - bp
Clarrisa Lanphear - bp
Mary Evans - bp, dis '37

Mary Witty - bp, ex '35
Roda Green - bp, m, dis
Lucy *Beely - bp, ex '33
Hannah Green - bp
Prudence Ellis - bp, m
Vorhtie Ellis
Sarah Babcock - bp, m, dis
Hannah Benjamin - bp, m, gone
Else *Beeby - bp, ex '33

* Periodical index says Beebe

"In 1833 there are 126 members belonging to this church."
"The following joined in 1833"

p. 9
James S. Green - bp, rj
Thomas Hattas - dis

Charles Coon - gone, dis
Welcome Burdick - bp

p. 10 "The following around 1833"
Sally Ellis - bp, dis '37
Fanny M. Potter - bp, m Silas Stillman
Diademia Perry - bp, d '54
Nancy Potter - bp, alias Coon
Lois Babcock
Roena Drake - bp, dis

Huldah Potter - bp, m Stillman
Eunice Green - bp, dis
Mary Ann Vincent - bp
Electy Coon - dis
Lucinda Hattas - dis

p. 11 1834

Charles Benjamin - bp, d. Nov 20'44
Hamilton Hull - bp, dis 37
Ira W. Babcock - bp, rj
Joshua L. Babcock - bp, rj
William Baker - dis
Clarke Beebe - bp, expelled
David Vincent 2nd - rj '37
Joseph Bloomer - bp, dis
Elijah P. Lewis - bp

Leander W. Lewis - bp, dis
Samuel Head - bp, dis
Benjamin Perry - bp, rj 1858
Nathan Coon - bp, dis
Joseph Babcock - bp, rj
Nathan Whitford - bp, dis
Edward Vincent - bp, dis
Israel B. Lewis - bp, dis
William Bloomer - bp, ex

p. 12 1834

Barnabas Bloomer - bp
Jesse Saunders Sr - bp, d
Amos Coon - bp, dis
Silas Benjamin Sr - bp, d '43
Matthew Ellis - bp, dis '37
Benjamin Green 2nd - bp, ex

Ezra Lanphere - bp, dis '52
Moses Cheesebrough - bp, rj
Rollin Head - gone to NB
Welcome Hill - bp, dis
Fitth Palmiter - bp, d '55
William Maxson - bp, d

p. 13

Elizabeth Lanphere - bp, d
Lydia Coon - bp, dis
Electa Coon 2nd - bp, dis
Susanna Hamiliton - bp, m Cottrell
Hannah Miner - bp, m. d '50
Ruth Benjamin - bp, d
Eliza Vincent - bp, dis
Arvilla Lanphere - bp
Lovina Chesebrough - bp, gone
Cinthy A. Witter - m York, d Mar 27'45
Emily Burdick Sterns - bp, dis

Maretta Warren - bp
Polly Vincent - dis
Rachel Green - bp
Charlotte Benny - bp, m, dis
Harriet Green Wilber - bp
Amy Benjamin - bp, d
Merily Whitford - bp, dis
Elizabeth Sanders - bp, dis
Betsey Burdick - d
Polly Burdick - dis '45

p. 14 Aug 17'34 "40 added & 2 dismissed; 186 members"

Calep Warren - d '95
Barton W. Millard - bp, dis
David Place - bp
Paul C. Witter - bp, rj
Paul Witter - d
Henry Saunders - bp, dis
George Lewis - bp, dis

Henry Y. Greenman - bp, dis '36
Erastus A. Green - bp
Stillman Palmiter - dis
Hermon Perry - bp, ex
John Perry - bp, ex '33
William Vincent - dis

p. 15 Jun 28'37: 178 members; Jun 10'38: 168 members

p. 16 1839

Samuel Witter
Daniel G. Vincent - bp
Horatio Maxson

Joshua Vincent - dis
Charles Maxson

p. 17 1834

Eumare Warren - d Jun'55

1836

Mariam Tift - bp
Phebe Green - bp, absent
Judy Green - deceased
Jesteve Phebe Taylor - dis
Thankful Satterlee

Mary Greenman - gone
Marcy Burdick Emerson - bp
Charlotte Stillman - bp, dis
Jovah Norell Sward - bp, gone

1839
Moriah Hull - d 1842
Jane Youngs Benjamin - bp, d
Cloe Whitford - bp, dis
Diadamy Perry Wilber - bp
Lucinda Saunders - bp, dis

p. 18   1839 189 members
Marieta Maxson - bp, dis
Katherine Maxson - dis

p. 19   1840 153 members
Lucretia Vincent   1842
Olive Vincent - bp, d '47
Olive Maxson - bp
Vosti Ellis - (crosed out)
Emily Manroe - bp, rj   1843
Sally Davis Palmiter - bp
Nancy Hall Pratt - bp, ex
Ruth Hemphill Whitford - bp, dis
Katharine Saunders Hamilton - bp

p. 20
Horran Walter - dis
John R. Shaw - bp
Amos T. Burdick - bp, rj
Iry Lanphere - ex
James Grinwald - bp, rj
Eld. James H. Cochran - d
Horace Potter - (crossed out)

p. 21   1843
Sarah Langworthy - d '51
Minerva Lee Elliott - bp
Mary Saunders Lewis - bp, dis
Oliva Hall Green - bp

p. 22   Jun'43: 155 members; Jun '44: 144 members;
                Jun'45: 165 members; Jun '46: 181 members

p. 23   Jan 1845
Rial Wescot - bp
Thomas Hull - bp
Fidelllo Hull - bp, d
Franklin Wescot - bp, dis
Quincy Howel - bp, rj
Benjamin Burdick - bp
Silas Burdick
Horace Witter
Edward Emerson
Dea. Charles D. Langworthy

p. 24
Melissa Shaw - bp
Maryann Maxson - bp
Clarissa L. Lewis - dis
Ruby Witter
Polly Saunders - dis
Susan Langworthy - d '51
Clarissa Kenyon - dis '50

Dorcas Saunders - bp, dis
Elizabeth Smith Hall - bp
Maritta M. Green - bp, dis
Amy Bentley - bp, dis

Susan Vincent - bp, d
Samantha Maxson - dis

Rachel W. Ellis - dis
Jane Green - dis

Maranda Youngs - bp, dis
Julia Grinald - bp, gone
Barbary Davis - bp, d '51
Harriet M. Vincent - bp, dis
Nancy Green White - bp, dis

Jeremiah Green - dis, restored
William S. Burdick - bp, dis
James Elliott - bp, rj
Dea. John Langworthy - d
William Jones - bp, rj
Robert West - rj

Lucy Coon - bp, dis
Susan Lanphere - dis
Ann E. Babcock - bp, dis
Mercy Wescot - bp

Phineas K. Shaw - bp
Samuel Webb - bp, rj
Ira Saunders - bp, ex
Squire Smith - bp
Jay Humphrey - bp, dis
Lafayette Witter - bp
Enos P. Burdick
Nelson G. Gavit - dis
Selah Manroe - dis

Maryann Webb - bp, rj
Harriet Blake - dis
Eunice West - d
Fanny Burdick
Eunice Hall - d '50
Polly Demming

p. 25   **After Jan 20'31: first meeting held at the School House near Jeremiah Green"s**

p. 26   no members listed

p. 27   **1849**

Thomas Williams   Joseph Stillman

1850

Eld. Jared Kenyon - dis

1851

Darius Kenyon

1852

Welcome I. Burdick - bp, dis '53   Theisando Maxson - bp
Carmeron Saunders - bp   Maxson Lanphere Jr - bp, absent
Samuel T. Burdick - bp   Amos Cheesebrough - bp, dis
Andrew J. Allen - bp   Melvin Cole - bp
Clarke Wilber - bp, d '55   James Williams - bp
Ezra Lanphear - (crossed out)   Wesley Wilbur - bp, dis
Charles Burdick - (crossed out)

p. 28   **1849**

Lucinda Lanphere Sweet - bp, absent   Catharine Williams

Jun 1850: 243 members

1851

Mary L. Williams alias Shaw - bp   Delilah Kenyon

1852

Martha Ann Maxson - bp   Harriet Cleare - bp
Matilda Lanphear -bp, dis   Eunice Lanphear - bp
Catherine M. Burdick - bp   Lydia Claire Allen - bp
Amy Lanphear - bp, ex   Hannah Cheesebrough - bp, dis
Trey A. Shaw - (crossed out)   Sarah Saphronia Manroe
Lydia M. Langworthy - (crossed out)

p. 29   **1849**

George Green - bp   Charles W. Langworthy - bp, ab
Chester R. Shaw - bp   John Greenman - bp, dis
William B. Greenman - bp, dis   Isaac Lewis - bp
George Wescot - bp, ex '48   Joseph Saunders - bp
Levi Burdick - bp   Charles Sweet - bp, absent
Samuel Whitford   H. W. Benjamin - bp
Nathan Lanphear 2nd - bp, ex '49   Champlin West - bp, d '55
Joseph Manroe - bp, expelled '55   Washington Cook - bp, ex
Romine Shaw - bp   Reuben Emery - bp, dis
Gurdon Cook - bp, expelled '53 (1st name hard to read)   Charles Burdick - bp, ex '49, restored '52

p. 30

Hannah Shaw - bp   Maria Smith Lynch - bp
Amanda Burdick Lewis Cleare - bp   Roxana Emerson - bp
Lydia M. Shaw Langworthy - bp, absent   Maranda Hall Lewis - bp
Emmorilla Benjamin Eastman - bp   Annis Lanphear Langworthy - bp
Mary Ann Babcock Lewis - bp   Priscilla Lewis Hadsall - bp
Esther Hall Hardy - bp, absent   Matilda Green - bp
Emaline Converse - bp, dis   Hannah L. Hull - bp
Susan Langworthy - d '51   Maria Langworthy Whitford
Elizabeth Burdick Place   Mary Elliot Cook
Elizabeth Wood Burdick   Charity Burdick
Olive Manroe Green   Mary Frances Maxson - dis

p. 31   **1849**

Simeon Smith	Charles H. Greenman - dis
William Green	David Green - absent
Luke Green 2nd	Andrew J. Green
Daniel Cook	Justus Cook - ex
Stephen Burdick	Richard Jones
Ira W. Phelps - dis	Freeborn Hamilton
Freeborn W. Hamilton	Stillman B. Witter
James B. Langworthy	Jonathan Saunders
Jarius Maxson - bp, dis	Sylvanus Smith - bp, dis
Sylvanus Maxson - dis	Alvin A. Lewis - dis
Leland Cook	

p. 32   **1879**

Sarah Saunders - bp	Prudence Burdick
Celia Green absent	Julia Elliot - ex
Betsey Cook	Elizabeth Sweet
Sophia Deming Fish - bp, dis	Tacy Hamilton Green - bp
Elizabeth Davis - (married name illegible)	Prudence Davis - d '50
Harriet Deming - dis	Emily Shaw Davis
Martha Jane Langworthy Benjamin	Electra Green Wooliver
Amanda Wood - dis	Arminda Cockran - dis
Sarah S. Hemphill Potter - bp	Mary Hamilton
Thankful Salina Satterlee Shaw	Laura Witter
Ruhanna Saunders	Mary Smith

p. 33   **1854**

Leroy Burdick

1853

Alvin A. Lewis - dis

1854

Daniel McComb Burdick	James Saunders
Milo Shaw	Joshua Green

p. 34   **1854**

Angelina Burdick -d '53	Tamer Smith - dis
Olive Burdick Allen - bp	Hannah Burdick - bp
Adeline Hall - bp	Elizabeth Burdick - bp
Salinda Burdick - bp	

CRR 1961.1.2   vault
Alfred Station
1831--1st Book   **IMS:1994**

2nd Book

Members of the Alfred Station SDB Church
Revised 1858

p. 1
Dea. Amos Burdick - dis '77
Paris Green - d
Dea. Nathan Lanphear - dis Andover '71
Jonathan Lanphear - dis Andover '71
Clark Green - nr, d
Edward Green - ex, restored '71, dis Andover '71
Jason Beebe - dis Andover '71, d
Asa Green - ex '62
Joshua Green - nr, d '63
Darius Satterlee - dis Nov '77
Elijah Lewis - d June 4'67
Welcome B. Burdick - exp '61, restored '71
Elijah P. Lewis - dis Feb '69
William Maxson - d
Erastus A. Green - dis '58
David M. Place - ex Jul'59
Daniel G. Vincent - ex Oct'59
John R. Shaw
Rial Wescot - ex Aug 11'61
Phineas K. Shaw - d May'86
Thomas Hull - d Nov '64
Squire J. Smith - d
Benjamin Burdick - d Jan'57
Samuel Witter
Layfayette Witter - ex Feb '63
Silas Burdick ex, d '69
Enos P. Burdick - ex, d Sep '75
Louis Babcock - dp '76
Susannah Cottrell - nr, d Nov'78
Martin E. Emerson - dis '62
Dea. Charles Langworthy - d June 9'76
Mercy Lovinia Emerson - d '59
Thankful Satterlee - d '74
Phebe Green - d '86
Lucretia Vincent

p. 3
Charles Wilber - dis '57

Fernando Maxson - exp Apr'64
Cameron Saunders - dp
Maxson Lanphear Jr - nr WI
Samuel P. Burdick - dis '82
Andrew J. Allen - dp
Melvin Cole - dp '72
James Williams - d Dec'62
Amos Shaw - dis '78
George Green - ex '62
G. W. Langworthy - ex Mar '66

p. 2
Cynthia Lanphear - dis 1st Alfred '70
Lydia Burdick - dis Feb'67
Eliza Hall - d Jul'66
Caty Burdick - d '59
Lydia Green - d '65
Olive Maxson
Polly Green - d '83
Anna Green Place
Mary Davis - d Sep'64
Celia Babcock - d '61
Clarissa Beebe - dis Andover '41
Sally Palmiter
Susan Lanphear - dis Andover '41
Avilda Hemphill - d May '84
Esther Lanphear - dis Andover '71
Huldah Hull Witter - nr '76
Hannah Green - dp '76
Anna Monroe - d Sep'74
Vasta Ellis - d '63
Prudence Stillman - ex Mar'70
Sally Lewis d Jan'69
Fanny M. Stillman
Huldah Stillman
Diadama Wilber - dp '76
Mary Ann Green - dis '59
Nancy Coon - d
Horace G. Witter
Emmorrilla Green Butler
Rachel Green - ex Mar'60
Harriet Wilber - dis '57
Thomas Williams - dis Scio
Joseph Stillman
Darius Kinyon - d Oct'66
P. G. Witter - ex

p. 4
Sally Julia Grinnell - nr
    d Dec 13'71 Kent OH
Minerva Elliott - dp '76
Oliva Green - dis Andover '71
Mercy Wescott - d '82
Kersiah Burdick - d Feb'80
Malissa Shaw - d Apr'87
Polly Deming - dis Andover
Ruby Witter - d '70
Fanny Burdick - prob w/o Enos P.
Lucinda Lanphear Sweet - dis
Maria Whitford - d '61

Catherine M. Burdick Cartwright - ex '63
Chester R. Shaw - ex Jul'59
Isaac M. Lewis
Charles Burdick - dp '70
Joseph Saunders - ex Jul '59
Levi S. Burdick
Charles Sweet - dis '63
Samuel Whitford
H. W. Benjamin - d May 3'61
Romain Shaw - ex
Simeon Smith - dis '59
William Green - ex Mar 10'61
David Green - dis '66
Luke Green - d Aug'87
Andrew J. Green
Daniel Cook
Stephen Burdick - dis '57
Richard Jones - dp May '72
Freeborn Hamilton - d Oct 8'69
Dea. F. W. Hamilton
Stillman B. Witter - ex '71, restored '71
James B. Langworthy - d Apr '86
Jonathan Saunders - dis Jun'63
Elsey Davis - dis Andover '72, ex Jul 1'59, restored '72
Hannah L. Hull Herrington - dis '62

p. 5

James I. Saunders
Joshua Green - dis Sep'85

1857

Osmund A. Burdick - bp, nr ,d '84
Dea. John T. Green - bp
Harrison W. Green - bp, ex May'87
Almerin G. Burdick - bp, dis '57
Elizabeth Burdick Wood - dis '65, restored Mar'78
Elno E. Burdick - bp, dis '57
Alvin A. Williams - bp, d '63
Samuel A. Wescott - bp, exp '70
John Burdick - bp
Tacy Green - dis Andover '71
Eliza Forbes - dis '60, d '84
Martha Jane Benjamin - d '80
Emily S. Davis
Sarah S. Potter - dis '68
Mary Hamilton - d June 29'64
Ruhama Saunders - dis Jun'63
Olive Allen - dis '65
Adaline Hall - d Feb '58
Salinda Burdick - d Nov'64
Mary Jane Lanphear - dis Andover '71
Fanny Stillman Shaw - bp

Daniel McComb Burdick
Lydia Allen - dp '76
Catherine Williams - d Sep'64
Mary L. Shaw - w/o J.R.
Delilah Kenyon - dis 1st Alfred '71
Martha Ann Maxson Allen - dis '68
Harriet Clair w/o J. Pettibone - dis
Einice Lanphear - ex
Tacy M. Shaw - d
Lydia M. Langworthy - ex Apr'65
Sarah Saphronia Manroe Hamilton - ex
Hannah Shaw Jaques
Amanda Clair - d '67
Lydia Maria Langworthy - ex
Emmorrilla Eastman - d
Maria Lynch - d
Annis Z. Langworthy - dis Andover '71
Roxana Emerson - dis Hebron '71
Mary Ann Lewis - dis Jan'69
Maranda A. Lewis
Leroy R. Burdick - dis '59
Orrilla Hadsall
Esther Hardy Hull - ex Jul'59
Matilda Coon - ex

p. 6

Milo Shaw

Mary Smith
Elizabeth Place - dis Andover '71
Mary A. Cook - dis Andover Sep'71
Mary Jane Shaw Lanphear - bp, ex
Alzina J. Langworthy - bp, d '59
Charity Burdick - dis '69
Olive Green
Sarah Collins - dis 1st Alfred '70
Prudence Burdick - exp Feb'63
Celia Green - WI
Betsey Cook
Elizabeth Sweet - d '72
Electa Woolever - dp '76
Thankful Salina Shaw - exp '60, d
Laura Witter -d
Marolla Burdick - bp
Hannah Burdick Saunders
Elizabeth Burdick - d '58
Orpha Green Burdick - bp, d Apr'83
Lovina Green - dis '66
Caroline S. Langworthy - bp, d'68

p. 7   **1857**

Eld. J. R. Irish - dis '58
David Vincent - d Jan '67

1858

Jesse Tefft - d Jan '61
Riley F. Burdick
Thomas Lewis - d '68
Alvin A. Lewis - dis '59
Dea. Daniel Potter - dis '55
William Riley Potter - dis '63
Charles Saunders - dis Aug'65
John C. Burdick
Finetta Saunders - dis '65

1859

John Vincent
Nathan Wardner - dis Jan'67
Nathan M. Lanphear - bp, dis Andover '71
Nathan Beebe - bp, dis Andover '71
Adrian Hemphill - bp, dis Feb
Joseph Vincent - bp
Alonzo Barber - bp
G. A. Williams - dis '68
Adelbert Potter - bp, '80
Asher Stillman - bp
Morton S. Wardner - bp, dis 67
Daniel Green
Luther Witter - d May '67
James Witter
Charles Shaw
George B. Shaw
Varnum Shaw - d Feb 18'65

1860

Ellen N. Burdick
Drusilla Witter Karr Green - bp
Ruby Witter - bp, dis Hartsville '72
Euphemia Witter Langworthy - bp
Lavinina Place - bp, d Apr'69
Harriet E. A. Cooper Bently - dis Scio
Lois Cooper Zeliff - bp, ex

p. 9   **1862**

Ella Vincent - bp, d '75
Sarah Davis - bp, ex '70
Ellen Williams - bp, dis Oct'87
Irena Palmiter - bp
Amanda C. Rudiger - ex Jun'64

1863

Irene Stillman - bp, d Apr'66
Huldah Stillman - bp, dis '87
Ency Potter Shaw - bp, dis
Otelia A. Shaw Merkt - bp
Orpha Babcock - bp, d Sep'78
Amelia Satterlee Burdick - bp, dis May '87

p.8

Charlotte Irish - dis '58
Amy Irish - dis '58
Freegift Vincent - d Feb '67

Adency Tefft
Matilda B. Burdick
Amanda Lewis - dis '61
Amanda T. Hamilton
Abagail Van Anthrop Vincent - d
Mary C. Lewis - dis '59
Martha Burdick - d '82
Rebecca Potter - dis '65
Caroline S. Burdick

Olive B. Wardner - dis Jan '67
Emma Satterlee - bp, d Oct 17'76
Ezra Potter - d Dec '78
Julia Satterlee Ormsby - bp, dis '83
Frances Williams Colegrove - bp
Elizabeth Nichols - bp
Genette Nichols - bp, exp '71
Calista Barber - bp
Sarah Barber - bp
Varania A. Manroe Hemphill - bp, ex
Polly Green - bp, dis May'87
Sarah Davis Manning - bp
Joseph Hull - dis '75
Lewis Manroe - ex, res
Leander Place
Henry Shaw - d

Doritha Sweet - bp, dp
Lois Hull - bp, d
Fanny M. Burdick Stillman - bp, d
Izora Manroe Crandall - bp
Mary Woodruff - bp
Hannah E. Shaw

Lavinnina Burdick Barber - bp
Mary Swift - bp
Almira Stillman
Content Potter

Sardinna Stillman Whitford - bp
Susan E. Burdick Maxson - bp, dis '77
Arvilla Potter - bp, dis Apr'65
Augusta Rudiger - bp, dis Jun'66
Francis S. Burdick - bp, d '50

Elizabeth Hemphill Beckworth - bp
Rebecca Rudiger - ex '68
Elliner Vincent - dis May '66
Phebe Sherman
Alzina Shaw

p. 10   1863
Max Rudiger - bp, ex Jun '66
Luther Lewis - bp, dis '82
Chancy Witter - bp
Halsey M. Burdick - bp, exp '76
George Palmiter - ex '82
Charles Wilbur - dis May'64

p. 11   1865
Anson P. Saunders - ad, dis '87
James Burdick - bp '64, dis Oct '65
Russell W. Burdick - bp, d '80
Raswell Emerson - bp, dis Apr '69

                     1866
William Shepherd - dis Mar '66
Lyman H. Lewis - dis May '67, d Sep 29'70
Thomas Tefft - ex May'72

p. 12   1863
Harriet Wilbur - dis May'64
Rhoda Wilbur - dis May'64

                     1865
Ida Long Kenyon - dis
Sophia Saunders Whitford
William Saunders - d
Saphrona Green
Cynthia Wells
Julia Bentley
Malvinia Burdick
___?___ Harmon

                     1866
Effie E. Forbes - bp, d Apr'69
Torcy Antoinette Shaw - bp
Elizabeth Cottrell
Latrie Potter - bp, dis
Mary Stillman - bp
Adelia M. Rogers - dis Jun 9'69

p. 13   1869
L. R. Swinney - dis '80

                     1871
Isaac Fenner - d Apr'87
Stillman B. Witter - d
Russell Green - bp, dis Andover
Fones J. Perry - bp, dis '81
Oliver D. Burdick - bp, dis Andover
Augustus Burdick - bp, dis Andover
Maxson Green - bp, dis Andover
Charles Forbes - bp
Albertus Hunt - bp
Cyemis Perry - bp
Charles Manroe - bp

Mary Jane Burdick
Catherine Witter Green
Lydia Witter - d Aug'86
Julia T. Palmiter
Polly Burdick - d

Charles L. Rudiger - bp, ex '68
Elberton Potter - bp, dis Apr'65
Eugene Rudiger - bp, ex Jun'66
James S. Babcock - bp
Silas Stillman
Christopher Tefft - d '83

Adelbert Potter - dis '64
Charles Vincent - bp
James Ferrell - bp, dp

Walter Shaw - ex, restored '87
Benjamin T. Rogers - dis Jun '69
Lucius Tefft

Harriet Wilbur Jr - dis May'64
Caleslee R. Root - dis

Sarah Cottrell - bp
Amelia Burdick - dis May '66
Jane Saunders - dis Aug '81
P. Amelia Saunders - dis Apr'79
Lydia Wilber - (crossed out)
___?___ Howell dis '69
Josephine Burdick - bp, dis May'66
Adelia Crandall - dis May'66

Florence Rose Shaw - bp
Medora Terrell - bp
Olive Potter - bp, d Jun 27'68
Adeline Wilber - bp, dis
Anna Witter - d '73
Martha Crandall

Welcome B. Burdick - dis, res
Phineas A. Shaw - bp
Herbert Hardy - bp, dis
William Langworthy - bp
Varnum Hull - bp, dis Andover
Clark Burdick - bp, dis Andover
Delmont S. Burdick d May'77
Daniel Langworthy - bp, dis Andover
George Cook - bp, dis Andover
William Sheriff - bp, ex '76
Edward Green - dis

Ezra M. Bennett - bp, dis Mar'83
William Ferris - ex, restored '80
Martin V. Barber - bp
F. M. Beyece - bp '76
Alvin Hall

p. 14
Amelia Fenner - d '72
Sarah Turner Green - d '81
Jennie Witter Cartwright - bp
Mary Thayer - bp, dis Richburg
Adaline Green Lewis - bp, dis
Ella Palmiter Cornish - bp
Nancy Thomas Livermore - bp
Frances Langworthy - bp, dis Andover '71
Phebe Burdick - bp, dis Andover '71
Agnes Burdick - bp, dis Andover '71
Sarah Hamilton Pease - bp
Angelica Manroe Wright - bp
Mrs. J.P. Hamilton
Mrs. Mary Barber - bp
Mrs. Stephen Clark - bp, ex '87
Minnie Palmiter - bp

p. 15 **1878**
Halsey F. Hadley
Sylvanus Whitford - bp
Ellsworth Edwards - bp
Lemuel Butterfield - bp, ex '80
Marcus McHenry - bp
A. Wheeler Davis - bp
Walter G. Ormsby - bp
Cushing W. Lewis - bp
A. G. Hadsell - bp
Herbert Hadsell - bp
Lemual Colgrove - bp, ex '81
Benjamin F. Gardiner - bp
William Hannan - bp, dis '82
Rowland Smith - bp
Willis R. Woodruff - bp
Satterlee Ormsby - bp
Willie S. Edwards - bp
Edward E. Hamilton - bp
Albert V. Potter - bp
James Hemphill - bp
Ed. D. Shaw - bp, ex '81
Francis Vincent - bp
Byron Smith - bp, ex '80
Charles Merkt - bp, ex '80
William Crandall - bp, ex '81
William R. Burdick - bp
Clayton Hadsell - bp
Loren Gridley - bp, ex '81
Erastus Bailey - bp, exp '90

Horace Edwards - bp
John P. Hamilton
Andrew J. Fenner
Eld. Charles A. Burdick - dis '78

1871
Eafosa Budick
Harriet Edwards - d '81
Harriet Green - bp, dis Andover '71
S. M. Swinney - bp, dis '80
Clara Hadsall - bp
Adell Shaw Hood - dis Hornell '86
Ellen Green - bp, dis Andover '71
Amanda L. Burdick - dis '78
Pamela Burdick - bp, dis Andover '71
Alice G. Carr - bp
Amy Sheriff - bp
Flora L. Manroe
Mrs. A.J. Fenner - bp, dis '82
Abbie Wells - bp, d '84
Dellie Palmiter - bp
Harriet M. Beyea - bp

p. 16
Verona E. Davis - bp
Betsey Hemphill - bp
Sarah Hemphill - bp
Lucretia Vincent - bp
Ella M. Shaw Conover - bp
Della Burdick - bp, dis '80
Minnie Beckworth Collins - bp
Cora D. Green - bp, d '80
Charlotte Thomas Harris - bp
Prudence Mc Henry - bp
Rosa M. Lewis Odell - bp
Frances Butterfield - bp, exp '80
Ella Perry - bp, dis '81
Brunette Thomas Whitford - bp
Ruth Hemphill Sherman - bp
Esther Fenner - bp
Frances Emerson - bp
Eva C. Keller Willard - bp
Mrs. Lucius Teft - bp
Eola L. Hamilton - bp
Ophelia Hemphill - bp
Florence Smith - bp
Rose Thomas Baird - bp
Dell Hadsell - bp
Ella Hall - bp
Minnie Thomas Abbott - bp
Augusta Lewis - dis '79
Lucy Barber
Mary E. Barber

p.17

William Barber
Silas Benjamin
Horace H. Thayer
Cyrenus Ormsby - bp, dis '83
Jennie Potter Wallace Roberts - bp
Mary Shaw Vincent - bp
Martha A. Thomas - dis '79
Mary Green Whitcomb - bp
Harriet C. Shaw Cook - bp
Delilah Rose - bp, dis '83

Joseph Edwards
Carrie E. Maxson - dis '83
Rev. D. E. Maxson - dis '83

Eliza R. Witter

Rev. James Summerbell
Frances Fuller - dis Apr'85

Warren Walker - dis '46
Edward Beebe - bp
Lorenzo A. Barber - bp
Lura A. Beebe
Bell Cottrell - bp
Almira Whitford - bp

p. 19
Thomas Brown Wardner - bp
Laverne Shaw - bp
Eugene Shaw - bp
John Lusk - bp
Frank Shaw - bp
Edward Green - bp
Melville Green - bp
Mils Palmer - bp
Jesse Monroe - bp
Floyd Hoffman - bp
Nathan Wardner - bp

1878

1879

1881

1883

1884

1886

1887

p. 18
S. Emogene Potter
Asenath Benjamin
Elizabeth Burdick - dis '81
Silas G. Thomas - dis '89
Adelbert Karr - bp, dis '89
William Ormsby - bp
Ed Palmiter - bp
DeAlton Ormsby - bp, dis '83
Esther Fisk - d Apr'82
Maria Vincent - bp

Hannah Maxson - dis '83
Dollie Maxson - dis '83

Frances E. Main

Roxana Fuller - dis Apr '85
Rachel Summerbell

Nettie Walker - dis '86
Nancy M. Frank
Polly Green
Susannah Cottrell - bp
Sarah Langworthy - bp
Luella Barber - bp

p. 20
Mary J. Austin
Sarah S. Wardner

Edna Green - bp
Elna Snyder - bp
Sarah Turner - bp
Winifred S. Beyea - bp
Flora Stillman - bp
Aggie Barber bp
Helen Witter - bp
Flora McHenry - bp
Justis Cook - bp
Jennie Green - bp
Vernon Barber - bp

Mar 11, 1872
List of Members dismissed to Andover

- Dea. Nathan Lanphere
- Mary J. Lanphere
- Jason Beebe
- Nathan L. Beebe
- O. Daniel Burdick
- Oliva Green
- Harriet Green
- George E. Cook
- Lucy Green
- Truman A. Burdick
- Agnes L. Burdick
- Frances Langworthy
- Jonathan Lanphere
- Polly Demming
- Phebe Burdick
- Susan Lanphere
- Nathan M. Lanphere
- Clarissa Beebe
- Welcome B. Burdick
- Varnum G. Hall
- Russel Green
- Mary A. Cook
- Edward Green
- Maxson A. Green
- Pamilia Burdick
- Annis Z. Langworthy
- Daniel Langworthy
- Esther Lanphere
- Clark Burdick
- Esther A. Green

CRR 1979.26.1 Vault
Alfred Station (2nd Alfred) SDB Church Records
1858-1887   IMS:1994

Hartsville SDB Church 1847-ca 1932
Hartsville Hill, Steuben Co, NY

CONSTITUENT MEMBERS

p. 6
Hiram Cornwell - dis '52
Charles W. Cornwell - dis
Amos R. Cornwell
Nathan Truman - dis
Ira W. Phelps
Daniel T. Burdick
Weeden Witter - d
Schuyler Whitford - dis
Jeremiah Burdick - dis
Silas Palmiter
George Palmiter - dis
James Neph
Elisha Potter - d
William D. Burdick - d Feb 14 '75
Joel Burdick
Hiram P. Burdick
David B. Satterlee - d

p. 7
Horace Palmiter
Alanson Potter
George Hood
Varnum Clark
Maxson W. Potter
Elisha Potter 2nd
Phineas S. Crandall - dis
A.L. Menney
Joseph L. Burdick
Lavinia Satterlee - dis
Susan Witter
Rorry Potter
Sabrina Cornwell - dis
Avis Hood

p. 8
John Witter - d
Widow Elizabeth Burdick - d '52
Hiram Palmiter
John Frankllin - ex
Jeremiah H. Burdick - dis
Andrew P. Satterlee - ex
Reuben Potter - d
Perry Potter
Henry Keller
J.B. Downs - ad '53, ex
Rebecca Witter - dis
Saphronia E. Potter
Mrs. Saphronia Potter

Sally Palmiter - d '52
Phebe J. Franklin - d
Hannah Cornwell - dis '52
Nancy Coon
Anna Davis - d '50
Sabrina Truman - d
Clarinda S. Wilcox - d '55
Catherine A. Truman - dis
Ashea M. Truman
Calista Witter
Mary Whitford
Hannah Neph - d
Hannah Burdick
Betsey Burdick
Emily C. Burdick - d '63
Cynthia Satterlee - d '63
Lina Clark - d

1852
Lydia A. Palmiter
Elizabeth Stone
Martha Satterlee
Locresia Satterlee - dis
Ellenor Satterlee - dis
Alvina Palmiter - d
Lavina Phelps
Sibil Burdick
Harriet Burdick
Roxy Potter
Louisa Witter
Lydia M. Cornwell - dis
Louisa J. Crandall - dis
Fanny Cornwell - dis '52

1852
Mary Clark
Catherine Witter - dis
Filena Potter - dis
Filena Palmiter
Almyra Potter
Mary Burdick
Sarah Burdick - dis
Nancy Burdick - dis
Anna Pettibone - d
Melissa Satterlee - dis
Eliza Potter - dis
Melvinia McDougal - d

p. 9
Thomas Bardeen - ad '52
Fanny Potter - '52, d Feb 9 '67
Alonzo Woodward - ad '56, dis
Alonzo Potter - ad '57
Langford Whitford - ad '57
Stillman Burdick - ad '57, excom
Russel Clark - ad '57
Cornelius Kettle - ad '57, dis
Nathan Forbs - ad '57, dis
Clark Hall - ad '57
Lewis Clark - ad '57, ex
Lyman Lewis - ad '57, dis
Lyman Lewis - ad '57, dis
Andrew Burdick - ad '57
A. F. Pettibone - ad '57
Samuel Burdick - ad '58
E. W. C. Kenyon - ad '62
Alanson Palmiter - ad '62
Mary E. Pettibone - b Feb 14 '37, d Mar 21 '60

p. 10 1863
John Grow - d
George Grow
Wells N. Burdick
John Gilbert - d
Syrus Cornice
G. O. Hood
Harrison Palmiter
William Burdick
William Pettibone
Jonathan Pettibone Jr - ad '65
Harrison Keller - '65
Walter Wilbur - ad '65, dis
Andy Burdick - ad '66
Olin Emerson - ad '66
William A. Hood - ad '66
Daniel Whitford - ad '66
E. Jonathan Allen - ad '69
Daniel S. Pettibone - ad '69
Sylvester Burdick - ad '69
Samuel Pettibone - ad '69
Miss Mirira Whitford - ad '66 (crossed out)

p. 12
H. G. Pope - ad '69
Sarah Burdick - ad '69
William Witter - ad '69
E. D. K. Davis - ad '69, dis
John Becker - ad '66, d
Elisha Edward Potter - ad '71
Darwin M. Potter - ad '71
James K. Pope - ad '75
Willie Bardeen - ad '75
Walter S. Hood - ad '75
Allie Burdick - ad '75

Nancy Keller - ad '53
Albina McCray - ad '52
Caroline Burdick - dis
Tacy Potter - ad '57
Polly Clark - ad '57, ex
Harriet Pettibone - ad '53
Euphemia Burdick - ad '57, dis
Mary A. Clark - ad '57
Mary McDougal - ad '57, dis
Elizabeth Burdick - ad '57
Nancy Pettibone - ad '57
Martha C. Lewis - ad '57
Mary Matison - ad '57, dis
Mrs. Downs - ad '58
M. E. Bryant - ad '58
Mrs. Prudence Burdick
Eliza T. McDougal - ad '62
Edward Emerson - ad '62
Serenus Allen

p. 11
Miss Martha T. Hood
Mrs. Huldah Grow - d
Mrs. Mary Grow Burdick
Miss Mary Ann Clark
Miss Avis Whitford
Mrs. Lavinda B. Burdick
Miss Charlotte E. Emerson
Mrs. Matilda B. Gilbert
Mrs. Thompson - d
Mrs. Mary Burdick
Mrs. Nancy Clark
Miss Almira E. Pope
Miss Lucina Witter
Miss Thankful Witter
Mrs. Tacy Keller
Mrs. Harriet Pettibone
Mrs. Angeline Pope
Miss Serena C. Keller
Mrs. Elizabeth Burdick
Elzora Chase - ad '66

p. 13
Mrs. Sarah Allen - ad '66, d
Miss Edna A. Pope - ad '66
Miss Alta S. Pope - ad '66
Miss Clara E. Leonard - ad '66
Rosa May Pettibone - ad '69
Miss Cleo Irene Burdick - ad ' 69
Miss Jennie E. Bardeen - ad '69
Mrs. Genett Burdick - ad '69
Mrs. Lucinda Davis - ad '69, dis
Catherine Burdick - ad '70
Mrs. Nancy Frank - ad '71

Fremont Whitford - ad '75
Elmer Burdick - ad '75
Frank Pettibone - ad '75
Ettie Pettibone - ad '75
Jennie A. Hood - ad '75
Harriet Whitford - ad '75

p. 14

Elder V. M. Babcock

Arminda Potter - ad '71
Alace Potter - ad '71, d '74
Oliva Pope - ad '75
Ruth Ann Pope - ad '75
Fanny M. Pope - ad '75
Isabella Burdick - ad '69

Mrs. Lucy Babcock

CRR 1984.8 vault
Hartsville NY SDB records
1847-1871 IMS:1995

ADDITIONAL BIOGRAPHICAL INFORMATION
(Some may be additional names or repetitative
particularly married names)

Allen, Prof. Jonathan - pastor 2 years, c. 1867
Babcock, Eliza Potter
Babcock, U. M. - pastor 1876-77, 1897-98
Bakker, Gerard H. - pastor 1976-1911; went home to Holland
Bardeen, Thomas - Deacon 1857, b Prattsburg Sep 3' 30, d Mar 3, 1911;
    m Libby L. Burdick Mar 5 '53
Burdick, Hiram P. - 1819-1914; b Alfred Dec 12'19, d Mar 28,1914;
    great grandson on his mother's side of Elder John Burdick of RI
    m Jun 19' 45 Emily C. Cook who d Mar 23'65, 4 children
    m 2nd Mary Bryant, M.D.
Burdick, Lester - Deacon 1907, later served Alfred
Burdick, Nancy - m Becker
Burdick, S. D. - (Stillman?)
Curtis, Mary Ann Clark
Cochran, J. H. - 1847 council for ordination of deacons
Cornwwll, Amos R. - instructor DeRuyter Institute, Albion Academy
Cornwell, Charles - deacon 1850
Cornwell, Elder Hiram - first pastor
Cotrell, Rev. Ira Lee - ordained 1879; pastor to 1880, 1899-1903
Crandall, Rev. Phineas - pastor one year
Davis, Rev. D.K. - 1869-75
Davis, Rev. John T. - 1890-94
Davis, Rev. H. Eugene - 1905-1907
Fisk, Rev. B. E. - 1880-85
Frank, Nancy - donated 2nd Alfred parsonage (?)
Goff, Rev. Ira - 1913-14
Greene, Maxson - served on 1847 ordination council of deacons
Grow, Grace - m ___?___ Burdick
Hood, George - ordained deacon 1865; b 1820-d 1886
Hood, Jennie - m ___?___ Whitford
Hull, Rev. Nathan V. - chairman of ordination council
Hutchins, Mrs. Edith
Hutchins, Rev. Jesse E. - 1907-1909
Jordon, Rev. Henry N. - pastor 1903-1909
Jordon, Mrs. Henry N.
Kalley, Rev. M. B. - pastor 1896
Kalley, Kate

Kenyon, Rev. W. C. - ordained 1863, served 1863-65
King, Clara Leonard
Maxson, Rev. Darwin E. - ordained 1853, served until 1856, 1885-1890
Merit, Susan Witter
Pettibone, Jonathan - deacon; b Jul 4'35, m Dec 3'57 Harriet C. Clair, d Nov 1, 1907
Polan, Mrs. H.L. (Ina)
Polan, Rev. Herbert - served 1912-13
Potter, Alonzo - deacon '50
Potter, Perry - called to deaconate 1856 but declined; donated land for Potter Cemetery
Potter, Eliza - (Babcock)
Roxy, Potter Ridfield
Rogers, B. F. - supply minister 1867
Shaw, Rev. George B. - served 1894-1895
Shaw, Dighton - served served 1898-99
Sheppard, Mark - supplied pulpit 1867
Simpson, Rev. William M. - pastor 1902-1911
Simpson, Mrs. William M. (Amelia?)
Smith, Stephen - ordination council of deacons 1847
Stillman, Olive Pope
Syndal, Cora B. Pope
Tomkins, Rev. George W.
Tomkins, Martha
Truman, A. M. or Nathan - ordained deacon 1847
Whitford, Silas - deacon 1907
Wilcox, Clarinda - (C. S. Willcox d 1855)
Witter, Susan - m Merrott
Woodward, Fannie Pope

This is a partial list compiled from a list copied by Rev. Albert N. Rogers, Historian, from card index supplied by Judson Stearns of Alfred Station NY.

CRR 1989.12   vault
Hartsville   IMS:1995

ed. note: Located at the corner of
Alfred Station Road and Landis Road;
it is now site of a new home.

Andover SDB Church 1871-1953
Andover, Allegany Co. NY

List of Ministers

A. H. Lewis...1871-72
T. R. Williams...1874-80
E. A. Witter...1883-85
Joshua Clarke...1889-93
Stephen Burdick...1897-03
Albert E. Webster...1906-09
Erlo E. Sutton...1911-12
Vernon L. Eggleston...1915-18
Carl Maxson...1948-51

T. L. Gardiner...1873
Jared Kenyon...1881-82
E. H. Socwell...1886-88
L. A. Platts...1894-96
Edgar D. Van Horn...1904-06
R. J. Severance...1909-10
A. Clyde Ehret...1912-15
Walter L. Greene...1918-46
Don A. Sanford...1951-1953

(First pastorate in conjunction with Independence for Sanford)

List of Deacons

Nathan Lanphear - d Apr 18 '79
William Bliss Clarke - d May 1 '96
Samuel P. Burdick - d Sep 14, 1914
Daniel L. Langworthy - d Apr 24, 1918

Welcome B. Burdick - d Apr 20 '90
John M. Mosher - d Apr 12, 1908
Henry Livermore
Edson C. Langworthy

p.300
Constituent Members

BURDICK:
- Welcome B. - acting deacon from 1871, ordained deacon 1879, d Apr 20 '90
- Oliver Daniel - s/o Welcome B. & Prudence Pettibone
- Truman Augustus - s/o Truman J. & Betsey Greenman of Newport RI
- Permelia - d/o Clark Green & Betsey Lanphear, w/o Truman A. d Feb 25, 1903
- Clark - s/o Green & Betsey, d Jan 20 '97
- Phebe - d/o Green & Betsey
- Samuel Lee - d York's Corners, Wellsville NY Apr 30 '97

BEEBE:
- Jason M. - s/o Seth & Elsie, d Oct 9 '72
- Clarissa - w/o Jason, d/o Nathan & Eunice Lanphear, d Aug 4 '84
- Nathan L. - s/o Jason & Clarissa, d Sep 1, 1904

CLARKE:
- Phebe - wid/o Hazard, d Mar 19 '73
- William Bliss - acting deacon 1871, ordained 1879, d May 1 '96
- Relief A. - w/o William B., d/o Nathan & Abagail Woodcock, d Feb 7 '99
- Frances - w/o Edson D., d/o Franklin & Annis Langworthy, d Mar 30, 1902

p. 301

Cook, Mary A. - w/o George Washington, d/o John & Sarah Elliot, d Oct 3 '84
Cook, George E. - s/o George W. & Mary; expelled for non-observance of the Sabbath Oct 14 '83
Crandall, William Wells, M.D. - united with SDB Church of Wellsville 1885, d Wellesville
Crandall, Euphemia E. - w/o William W., d/o Elisha & Miranda Maxson Potter
Davis, Leroy C. - d Jan 13 '99
Davis, Elsie - wid/o Henry, d 1880
Everett, Grace A. - w/o Edwin, d/o Hazard & Phebe Clarke, d Jun 27, 1901

GREEN:
- Edward - s/o Paris & Polly
- Tacy - w/o Edward, d/o Freeborn & Tacy Hamilton
- Maxson A. - s/o Edward & Tacy, d Aug 17, 1917
- Ellen A. - d/o Edward & Tacy, d Jul 29 '73

Olivia - w/o William, d/o Benajah & Catherine Hall
Russell P. - s/o William & Olivia
Harriet - d/o William & Olivia, w/o Menzo Wamsley, d Sep 28, 1905
Nora Livermore - w/o George A.; expelled for violation of covenant obligations, 1890

Hall, Varnum G. - s/o Benajah & Catherine, d Nov. 30, 1901

LANPHEAR:
Nathan - served many years as deacon of Alfred
recognized as deacon at organization of Andover Church, d April 8 '79
Susan - w/o Nathan, d/o Paris & Polly Green, d Oct 15 '83

p. 302
W. Mortimer - s/o Nathan & Susan
Mary Jane - w/o Virgil A. Willard, d/o Nathan & Susan
Jonathan - s/o Nathan & Eunice Satterlee, d Dec 30 '79
Esther - w/o Jonathan, d/o Seth & Elsie Beebe, d Mar 19, 1908
Ellen G. - w/o Oliver E. Vars, d/o Jonathan & Esther

LANGWORTHY:
Annis Z. - w/o Daniel Franklin, d/o Dea. Nathan & Eunice Lanphear
Daniel L. - s/o D. F. & Annis; ordained deacon Feb 13 '86
Agnes E. - w/o D. L., d/o T. A. & Permelia Burdick

Ware, Anna Louisa - wid/o Robert, adopt d/o William Bliss & Relief A. Clarke
Livermore, Clarissa - wid/o Maxson G., d/o Hazard & Phebe Clarke, d Jan 9, 1902

p. 303   **Admitted by Baptism**

BURDICK:
Addie Hofer - w/o Lavern, protege of William Bliss & Relief A. Clarke, bp Sep 14 '72
dis Aug '83, joined Friendship Church
Lucy - w/o Samuel Lee, d/o Orrin Turner, bp Apr 19, '73, d Mar 3 '84
Truman Green - s/o Truman A. & Permelia, bp May 8 '86, dis 1st Alfred
Emma - w/o Truman G., d/o Arnold W. & Sarah Saunders Collins, bp Nov 16 '89
dis 1st Alfred
Mary - w/o Samuel P. Burdick, bp Apr 9 '87
Jane W. - w/o Milo Palmer, d/o S. P. & Mary, bp Apr 9 '87, d May 18, 1901
Leroy - s/o S. P. & Mary, bp Apr 9 '87, dis 2nd Alfred 1900
Addie - d/o Oliver Daniel & Susan Davis, bp Jun 15, 1901
Susan - w/o Oliver Daniel, bp May 5 '94
Elma - d/o O. D. & Addie Fowler, bp Apr 9 '87, w/o Dayton
s/o Stillman M. & Catherine Burdick,

Baker, George - s/o Henry & Ellen, bp May 11 '89
Baker, Jennie - w/o Jesse Baker, d/o Henry & Ellen, bp May 11 '89
Beebe, Addie E. - w/o Nathan L., d/o Edwin Brown, bp Apr 19 '73
Clarke, Edson D. - s/o Jeremiah & Catherine, bp Sep 1 '83
Brown, Tolcott G. - s/o Edwin, bp Apr 9 '87, d Apr 8, 1909
Brown, Sophronia - w/o T. G., d/o Welcome & Prudence Burdick, bp Apr 9 '87

p. 304
Brown, Lena - w/o Melvin S. Collins, d/o T. G. and Euphemia, bp Apr 9 '87
Clair, Mary Jane - wid/o Lee A., bp Oct 20 '94, d May 4 '96
Collins, Melvin S. - s/o Arnold W. & Sarah, bp Oct 20 '94
Cartwright, Casner - s/o Leonard & Catherine Burdick, bp Oct 20 '94
Bozzard, Emma - w/o Clark W. Robbins, d/o William & Sarah, bp Sep 1'83

GREEN:
Mary A. - w/o Maxson A., d/o Cyrus N. & Ruisa Beebe Capen, bp Aug 1 '80
Euphemia Ella - d/o M. A. & Mary, bp Jan 24, 1902
Edgar - dis Mar 23, 1907

Mahala - w/o Edgar, dis Mar 24, 1907
    Edith - w/o Archie Hibbard, d/o Edgar & Mahala, bp Oct 20 '94
    Sherman - s/o Edgar & Mahala, bp Oct 20 '94, dis Little Genesee Feb 29, 1902
Hofer, Theodore - protege/o William Bliss & Relief A. Clarke, bp Aug 1 '80
Hall, Minnie - d/o Lewis & Elizabeth, bp Jul 2 '92, dis little Genesee
Hall, Bertha - w/o Bert Mead, d/o Lewis & Elizabeth, bp Jul 1 '93, joined M. E. Church of Olean
Lusk, Eliza M. - w/o John, d/o Green & Betsey Burdick, bp Apr 8 '87, d May 25 '89
Lusk, Charles Sumner - s/o John & Eliza M., bp Apr 9 '87

p. 305
LANGWORTHY:
    LaVerne Daniel - s/o Daniel L. & Agnes, bp Jul 1 '93
    Franklin Augustus - s/o Daniel L. & Agnes, bp Jul 1 '93
    Edwin, - s/o Daniel Franklin & Annis, bp Sep 1 '83
    Egbert Russell - s/o Daniel L. & Agnes, bp Jun 20 '96
    Marie Agnes - d/o Daniel L. & Agnes, bp Jun 20 '96
Irish, Flora - w/o Hervey Crandall, d/o George, May 12 '77
Moland, Maria - w/o Milo D. Morland, d/o Franklin & Annis Langworthy, d Jun 18 '83
SNYDER:
    Benjamin - s/o Sarah, wid/o Dea. Amos Burdick, bp May 21 '81, expelled for violation of covenant obligations Oct 19 '84
    Ida M. - w/o Benjamin Snyder, d/o Warren, gd/o Wid. Sarah Burdick, bp May '81, ex '94
    Elma - w/o Elmer Roberts, d/o Frank & Angeline, bp Aug '91, dis Scio Church
    Frank F. - s/o Wid. Sarah Burdick, bp May 5 '94
    Angeline - w/o Frank F., d/o Benjamin & Louisa Monroe Green, bp May 5 '94
    Edwin E. - s/o Frank F. & Angeline, bp May 5 '94

p. 306
Perry, Oscar - bp Apr 9 '87, d May 15, 1935
Potter, w/o Edward M., d/o Russell Burdick, bp Apr 9 '87, dis 2nd Alfred Feb 1900
Turner, Eli H. - s/o Orrin, bp Nov 16 '89
Witter, Agatha - d/o Paul C. & Susan, bp Aug 7 '80
Williams, Ida - w/o Joseph L., d/o Andrew J. & Catherine Witter Green, bp May 5 '94
Wamsley, Menzo - bp Nov 16 '89
Potter, Elinor - d/o Clark & Persis Ford, bp May 12 '87
Potter, Josephine - w/o Arthur Morland, d/o Clark & Persis Potter, bp Aug 3 '79, d Jun 20 '90

p. 312   Admitted by Letter
BURDICK:
    Silas G. - bp May 12 '77, ex Apr 2 '87
    Samuel P. - s/o Welcome B. & Prudence, ad May 7 '81; ordained deacon Oct 15 '90
    Martha A. - w/o Silas G., ad May 12 '77
    Rev. Stephen - s/o Enos P. & Frances Peckham, ad Mar '97; pastor 1897-1903
    Prudence - w/o Dea. Welcome B., ad Oct 27 '88, d Jun 17 '89
    Nora - w/o Dr. George E., dis Jun 1909
Beebe, Henry C. - d Apr 17 '91
Beebe, Harriet S. - w/o H. C., d Aug 8, 1910
Beebe, Lovina - w/o John, d Apr 5 '94
Bowers, Eunice - w/o William, d/o Jonathan & Esther Lanphear, d Aug 3 '84
Backus, Lucy A. - wid/o Rev. J. E. N. Backus
CLARKE:
    Helen - wid/o Decatur M., ad Sep 14 '89, d May 12 '92
    Rev. Joshua - ad Sep 15 '88, pastor 1889-93, dis Feb 10 '94, d while pastor of First & Second Verona, Oneida Co. NY Feb 9 '95; 54 active ministry
    Esther L. - w/o Joshua, ad Sep 15 '88, d May 21 '92 Alfred NY
    Carrie Evans - w/o Joshua, d/o Gurdon Evans, A. M., dis Feb 10 '94

Coon, Aaron Welcome - s/o Aaron, ad Nov 3 '88, dis July '92
Coon, Tacy - w/o AW., d/o John Stearns & Elizabeth Burdick Stearns, ad Nov 3 '88, dis Jul '92

p. 313

Baker, Angeline - d/o John S. & Sarah Olds
Baker, Ellen - wid/o Henry, ad Jul 11 '88
Baker, Sarah - d/o Henry & Ellen, ad Jul 11 '88
Baker, Susan - d/o Henry & Ellen, ad Jul 11 '88, d Nov 26, 1906
Sullivan, Abraham Wolfe M. D. - ad Sep 22 '88
Sullivan, Della May - w/o A. W., d/o William L. Catlin, ad Sep 22 '88
Perry, Phebe - w/o John G., d/o Weeden Witter, ad Sep 29 '88, d Dec 19, 1901
Witter, E. Adelbert, - s/o Charles H. & Abbie K. Edwards Witter;
 unanimously called as minister by this church, ordained Dec 2 '82;
 served until 1885
Witter, Mary Benjamin - w/o Rev. E. A., d/o Samuel & Helen Benjamin
Clarke, ad Jan 28 '83, d Niantic RI Jan 27 '89
Witter, Frank - s/o Weeden
Witter, Lillian - w/o Frank, d/o Andrew & Leydia Allen, ad Jan 19 '89, d Nov. 25, 1910
Potter, William Maxson - ad Nov 10 '88, d Oct 19 '90
Potter, Sophronia - w/o William, d/o Fitch Palmiter & Maria Burdick, ad Oct 19 '90
Redfield, Roxie Potter - wid/o Harvey, ad Oct 19 '90, d Jun 20, 1910
Remington, Delos D. - ad Sep 14 '99, d Apr 2, 1925
Remington, Philena - w/o D. D., ad Sep 14 '99

p. 314

Turner, Sarah - w/o Eli H., d Jul 25, 1916
Socwell, Rev. Eugene Herbert - pastor 1886-88
Socwell, Matilda - w/o Rev. E. H.
Hall, Benajah
Hall, Lewis - ad Sep 20 '90, d Feb 12 '92
Hall, Elizabeth - w/o Lewis, ad Sep 20 '90, d Sep 4 '97
Hall, Catherine - w/o Varnum G., d/o Dea. W. B. & Prudence Burdick,
 ad Sep 15 '88, d Oct 6, 1901
Wheaton, Louisa - wid/o Seeley, d/o Weeden Witter; admitted on profession of faith
 & resumption of Sabbath observance Sep 15 '88

CRR 1957.3 vault
Andover NY SDB Church Records
1871-1953 IMS:1995

Independence SDB Church 1824-1975
Independence Valley, Allegany Co. NY

The first SDB's in about 1818 belonged to First Alfred parish. It was first set off from First Alfred in 1824. It deminished until about 1830. In 1833 eighteen people petitioned First Alfred to become a branch. It was reoganized in 1824. (The account of this can be found in First Alfred's records and The SDB Missionary Magazine.)

The building was sold in 1973 to the Mennonites. In 1975 it merged with Second Alfred.

Constituent Members

John P. Livermore
Annis Greene Livermore w/o J. P.
Tacy Fitch Livermore w/o Edmund
Clarissa Brown Tanner w/o John
Thankful Stillman w/o Nathan
Betsey Bassett Green w/o I. W.
Phebe Whitford Clarke w/o H. P.
Mr. & Mrs. Nathan Merritt
Jonathan Davis
Mr. & Mrs. Scholard Babcock

Edmund Livermore
Mr. & Mrs. William Hamilton
John Tanner
Nathan Stillman
Isaiah W. Greene
Hazard P. Clarke
Icabod Babcock
Sally Babcock w/o Icabod
Anna Clarke Davis w/o Jonathan
Peleg Babcock (Madison Co NY)
Lucinda Brown Babcock w/o Peleg

List made by former pastor Rev. William L. Burdick about 1904 when he checked with those living whose memory went back to the time of the organization.

List of Pastors

Stillman Coon 1834-40
Decatur M. Clarke 1841-45
Sherman S. Griswold 1845-48
Thomas E. Babcock 1848-55
Jared Kenyon 1855-80
Ira Lee Cottrell 1880-83
Gideon H. F. Randolph 1883-84
J. E. N. Backus 1885-86
Herman D. Clarke 1887-93

Madison Harry 1893-95
William L. Burdick 1896-1904
Alonzo G. Crofoot 1904-11
Leslie O. Greene 1911-14
Walter L. Greene 1914-43
Zack White 1944-45
C. Rex Burdick 1945-46
Carl Maxson 1947-51
Don A. Sanford 1951-55

Deacons of the Church

Nathan Merritt 1834-37 or 38
William Slocum Livermore 1838 or 1839-99
Daniel S. Remington 1838-39, 1856, 1876-88
Archibald G. Coon 1857-65

Asa C. Burdick 1865-70
Sherman G. Crandall 1870-1918
Devillo E. Livermore 1894-
C. Milford Crandall 1918-

History of the First Seventh Day Baptist Church
of Independence NY 1824, 1834-1934 **B-file**
prepared by Walter L. Greene, D. D.

Members from Oct. 4, 1845

p. 129

John P. Livermore
William S. Livermore
Nathan Stillman - d Apr 24 '63
Isaiah W.. Green - d Oct 18 '64
Nathan Maryott
William B. Clark - dis Jan 13 '72
John C. Bassett - d Jan 12 '52
Dea. Samuel B. Clark - d
Stephen Clark
Amos Kenyon
Decatur M. Clark - ad Aug 16 '35
Leroy C. Davis - ad '35, dis Jan 14 '72
H. P. Clark - ad Oct '35, d Dec 25 '63
Charles Eaton
Daniel S. Remington - ex Aug 30 '56, res Ap '76
Edmund Livermore
Philarmon Livermore - ad Dec '36, dis Jul '49
Barliss S. Bassett - ad Jan '37, dis Jun '77
Annis Livermore - d
Amanda Livermore w/o J.P.L.
Hannah Stillman
Betsey Green w/o I. W. - dis Dec 29 '74
Tacy E. Green - dis May 5 '55
Nancy Maryott - dis Jan 9 '58
Phebe Clark w/o H. P. - dis Jan 14 '72
Laura Clark
Olivia Clark - dis '48
Martha Bassett
Maria C. Green - d Dec 2 '62
Eliza Clark
Sally Clark
Eliza Remington
Tacy Livermore w/o Edmund - d May 31 '75
Sarah Stillman
Miranda Wood
Mary Maryott
Azuba Clark

p. 130

Dea. Stenet Crandall - bp Sep '42, ex Nov '53
Joseph Potter
Jerome B. Remington - bp Apr 1 '43, ex
Henry Crandall
Nathaniel Perkins Jr - bp Mar 2 '44, ex Nov '54
William Perkins - ex Jan 21 '49
Elisha B. Green - ex Sep 8 '50
George Rosebush
Walter B. Slingerland - ex Aug 14 '46
Edmund D. Potter
Noah Levins - ex Jan 21 '49
Nelson Wood - ex Apr 19 '46
Allen S. Livermore - ex Jan 18 '54, rest Jan '71
Elias Wells - d Nov 30 '70
John Brown - ex Jan '49
Alexander Perkins - ex Jan 3 '49
William B. Green - d Dec '60
George C. Reynolds - ex Feb 3 '50
Fanny Remington - ex '61, d
Selucia Clark
Almira Steward - ex Jan 9 '58
Martha M. Stillman - dis Dec 26 '47
Grace Ann Clark - dis Jan 14 '72
Arminda Livermore - dis Jul 22 '76
Eliza Crandall
Eliza Perkins - ad Feb 20 '41
Minerva Slingerland - ad Feb 27 '42, ex Jun 1 '62
Harriet Wells - ad May '41
Mrs. C. Card - ad Oct '41, d '67
Julia A. Bassett - bp Apr 1 '43
Cordelia Haseltine - ad Feb 26 '44
Eliza Reading - bp Apr 1 '43
Olive Perkins - ad Mar 20 '44
Lucretta Perkins - bp May 3 '44, d Mar '60
Cloe Ann Perkins - bp Mar 3 '44
Martha Crandall
Amorilla Rosebush - ad Mar 10 '44, ex Sep 8 '50

p. 131

William Rosebush - ex Jan 21 '49
Asa C. Burdick - ad Apr '44, dis May 5 '55
Sherman S. Griswold - dis Jan 20 '47
Harvey W. Benjamin - ad Jan '46, dis '48
Alpheus A. Wood - dis Apr 11 '47
Edwin Griswold - dis Apr 11 '47
Leander Livermore - dis
Lee Lewis - d '47
Edwin Haseltine - bp Jun '47
Norris Crandall - bp Jun '47, ex Feb 15 '52
Thomas E. Babcock - Apr '47, dis Sep '55
Charles (George) L. - ad '49, ex Jun 11 '65
Rheuben Kelsey - ad Oct 27 '49, d Oct 2 '63
Wellington Kelsey - bp Oct 27 '49, d Sep '53
William S. Cottrell - ad Jul '49, ex Jun '62
Mary Jane Potter - d
Cordelia Livermore
Sophia Deming - dis '47
Martha A. Potter - d
Phobe Crandall
Julia Ann Reynolds - ex Feb 25 '55
Elizabeth Jane Slingerland - Jan 17 '64
Eveline Wells
Julia M. Stillman - d Feb 13 '54
Abagail A. Wells - dis Mar 10 '75

Kesia Crandall - d Mar '75
Alma Griswold - dis Apr 11 '47
Alma L. Griswold - dis Apr 11 '47
Mary Jane Potter
Mary Reading
Melissa Babcock - ad '47, dis Sep '55
Caroline Green - ad '49
Jane Brown - dis Jan 11 '65
Susan Slingerland - ad May '49

p. 132
Henry Stillman - ex Sep 8 '50, rest Jan 21 '81
Nelson R. Crandall - ad May '37
Barney Crandall - ad Sep 29 '38, d Feb 22 '69
Maxson G. Livermore - d Nov 29 '46
Pardon Green
Perry C. Potter
Jeremiah Clark
David Slingerland - ex Jan 17 '64
Joel Crandall - ad Jan 5 '39, d
Samuel Livermore - Jan 5 '39
John Livermore - ad Jan 5 '39
William Livermore - ex Mar 5 '65
John C. Green - dis Dec 29 '74, rest Jan 21 '81
John Bassett - ad Feb 30 '41, ex Jan 21 '49
Lucius Wood - ad Feb 27 '41, ex Apr 19 '46
Allen M. Wood - ad Feb 27 '41, d '56
Briggs B. Livermore
Charles Card - ad May '42, d
Joseph Crandall - ad Jun '42, Jan 21 '49
Mary Green
Rachel Paxton - ex Oct 14 '57
Nancy Green - dis Oct 9 '59
Mary Clark - d Feb 6 '47
Clarissa C. Livermore - dis Jan 14 '72
Caroline Clark
Susan Sole - d
Emily Clark - dis
Rebecca Reading - d
Olive B. Forbes - dis Apr 12 '59
Lavina Steward - dis
Saphena Slingerland - d
Eliza Livermore - ad Jan 5 '39, d Mar '53
Relief A. Clark - w/o W.B., ad May '40, dis Jan '72
Nancy Hall
Mary Livermore - ad Aug 5 '40, d '57
Densy Eaton - ad Jan 30 '41
Phoebe Kenyon - ex
Betsey Bassett

p. 133
J. D. Bennet - bp '57, Troupsburg
Rev Jared Kenyon - ad Jun 2 '55
Clarissa Kenyon - ad Jun 2 '55
Archibald G. Coon - ad Jul '55, dis '64

Phebe A. Coon - ad Jul '55
Amanda Stillman - ad Aug '56
Caroline D. Youngs - ad Aug '56, dis '58
James Youngs - bp '57, dis '88
Ruel Hamilton - bp '57
Ira Crandall - bp '57
James Crandall - bp '57, dis Nov 15 '69
Adelbert Stillman - bp '57, Jan 17 '64
Elias Hall - bp '58, ex May 5 '65
Uriah Davis - bp '58
William A. Clark - bp '58
Edelbert Eaton - bp '58
Lester Eaton - bp '58, d '62; fell for freedom
Robert Voohees - ad '59, ex May 27 '64
Henry Clark - ad May '60
Mrs. Belinda E. Livermore - bp Feb 26 '53
    ex Nov 5 '54, rest Jan 20 '71
Emeline L. Livermore - ad May 6 '54
Amarette Fish - bp Oct 21 '54
Clarissa Kenyon - ad Jun 2 '55
Flavia Page - ad Oct 21 '54
Phebe A. Coon - ad Jul '55, dis '64
Amanda Stillman - ad Aug '56
Caroline D. Young - ad Aug '56, dis '68
Mrs. J. D. Bennet - bp '57
Marcell Crandall - bp '57
Hannah Livermore - bp '57, dis Jan 14 '72
Flora Livermore - bp '57
Lovina Green - bp '57, dis Aug 21 '74
Mary Wells - bp '57, dis Feb 6 '75
Sarah Hamilton - bp '57
Sophena Lewis - bp '57, d '64
Louisa McCarn - bp '57, d Apr 16 '72
Jane Rosebush - bp '58
Ora Mariah Hall - bp '58

p. 134
Charles H. Clark - bp '60
Leroy Clark - bp '60
Sherman G. Crandall - bp '60, d May 9, 1918
William R. Crandall - bp '60, d Nov 1920
Charles H. Langdon - bp '60, ex Jun 14 '68
Almond C. Crandall - bp Jan 24 '60, ex Jun '64
Edwin Stillman - bp Jan 24 '60,
    d is Mar 5 '69, rest Jun 5 '76
Charles Voorhees - bp Apr 23 '61
Henry Knox - ad Apr 23 '61, d Feb '63
Daniel T. Graves - bp Jun 9 '61
William Lasher - bp Jun 9 '61
Asa C. Burdick - Jun 10 '65, dis Aug 20 '70
Charles E. Green - bp Dec 15 '66
Maxson Crandall - bp Dec 15 '66
Arthur Eaton - bp Dec 22 '66
William Williams - bp Dec 22 '66

Gurden Green - ad Apr 11 '68
Franklin Green - ad Apr 11 '68
Chester Green - ad Apr 11 '68
Valorus Graves - ad Apr 11 '68, d Apr 20, 1931
Augusta Voorhees - ad '59
Antoinett Potter - ad '59
Mary E. Voorhees - ad '60
Mrs. Henry Clark - ad Jul '60
Sarah A. Livermore - bp '60
Amelia N. Clark - bp '60
Almira N. Crandall - bp Jun 24 '60
Anna Clark - bp Jun 24 '60, dis Jan 14 '72
Josephine Eaton - bp Jun 24 '60
Celia Green - bp Jun '60
Mrs. Ellen Baker - bp Jun '60
Sally Ann Potter - ad Aug 17 '60
Mrs. Uriah Davis - ad Aug 17 '60
Betsey A. Voorhees - bp Apr 20 '61, d '61
Minerva Knox - bp Apr 20 '61
Adella Parker - bp Apr 20 '61
Jane Parker - bp Apr 20 '61, rest
Betsey Knox - ad Apr 20 '61
Mrs. Fanny Hazeltine - bp Aug 26 '62

p. 135
___?___ Knox - ad Apr 11 '68
___?___ Knox - ad Apr 11 '68
Delos Crandall - ad May 2 '68, dis Nov 7 '68
G. Westley Rosebush - bp Jan '71, d Jan 22, 1926
Herbert M. Clarke - bp Jan 21 '71, d Oct 1933
Elsenette Clarke - bp Jan 21 '75
Nancy Buyer - bp Jan 21 '71, ex
Hellen Clark - bp Jan 21 '71
Emily B. Crandall - bp Jan 21 '71, d May 9, 1920
Mary P. Benjamin - bp Jan 21 '71
Julia Livermore - bp Jan 21 '71
Mary Remington - bp Jan 21 '71
Alice E. Clarke - bp Jan 21 '71
Frank Potter - bp Jan 21 '71
Adelbert Wood - bp Jan 21 '71
Oscar Remington - bp Feb 11 '71
Henry K. Bassett - bp Feb 11 '71
Adelwin M. Green - bp Feb '71, dis Mar 8, 1930
John Green - bp Feb 11 '71
Mrs. Augustus Davis - bp Feb 11 '71
Mrs. William Lasher - bp Jun 9 '61
Mrs. Daniel T. Graves - bp Jun 9 '61
Mary Ann Knox - bp Jun 9 '61
Lucy McKune - bp Aug 8 '63, d May '66
Tacy E. Burdick - ad Jun 10 '65, d Aug 20 '70
Ellen M. Burdick - ad Jun 10 '65
Caroline Brown - ad Jun 10 '65
Mrs. Elvira Williams - bp Dec 22 '66
Rocelia Rosebush - bp Dec 29 '66

Emma Rosebush - bp Dec '66, d Apr 23, 1927
Emmegene Green - bp Jan '67, d Feb 11, 1929
Ida M. Burdick - ad Jan 12 '67, dis Aug 20 '70, rest Jun 5 '76
Arminda Hazeltine - ad Feb 15 '76
Esther Bassett - Apr 11 '68
Susan Potter - May 9 '68
Alvira Lee - ad May 30 '68
Lucy Davis w/o Leroy - ad 1866, dis Jan '72

p. 136
Mary Chapman - ad Feb 11 '71
Edsil Socker - by acclimation of faith Feb '71
Ann Green - ad Feb 25 '71
Devillo Livermore - ad Feb 25 '71
Nellie Green - ad Feb 25 '71, dis Jun 6 '72
Luther Green - by acclimation of faith Feb '71
Richard A. Jacobs - bp Jul 27 '72
Dora Wood - bp May 16 '74
Frank Hill - bp Apr 15 '76
Allie Glover - bp Apr 15 '76
Lewis Morgan - bp May 15 '76, dis
Lizzie Green - bp Apr 15 '76, d Feb 7, 1926
Edwin A. Stillman - ad Jun 5 '76
Ida M. Stillman - ad Jun 5 '76
Miss Clara Stillman - bp Jun 15 '76

p. 137
William Reynolds - ad Mar '51, d Oct 4 '54
David W. Wells - ad Apr 17 '52, dis Sep '55
Edwin Burdick - ad Jun 18 '52, dis Mar '58
Manin Livermore - bp Feb 12 '53
Albert Hazeltine - bp Feb 12 '53,, d Aug 11 '64
Pardon Wells - bp Feb 12 '53, d for country '62
Albert Green - bp Feb 12 '53, dis Aug 21 '74
Francis Bassett - bp Feb 12 '53
Marion Wood - bp Feb 12 '53
Delancy Crandall - bp Feb 12 '53
Ethan T. Green - bp Feb 26 '53, d in the army
Franklin Green - bp Feb 26 '53, d 1861
Franklin Davis - bp Feb 26 '53
Deloss Remington - bp Feb 26 '53
Jeremiah Reading - bp Feb 26 '53
Simeon B. Card - bp Jun 10 '54; Troupsburg
Erastus H. Fisk - bp Jun 10 '54, d in the army; (Troupsburg)
George W. Page - bp Jun 10 '54; (Troupsburg)
Hannah Kelsey - ad Oct '49, d Dec 19 '65
Elizabeth Kelsey - bp Oct 27 '49, d
Mary Bassett - bp Nov 3 '49, dis Mar 17 '60
Lydia Reynolds - ad Mar '51, d Jul 20 '51
Mrs. Lorana Stillman - ad Feb 21 '52
Emily Green - ad Feb 28 '52, dis Dec 29 '74
Katharine Wells - ad Apr 17 '52, dis Sep '55
Ellen E. Babcock - ad Apr '52, dis Sep '55

Mrs. Mary Burdick - ad Jun '52, dis, d
Miss Maria Wells - bp Feb 11 '53
Sarah Bassett - bp Feb 11 '53, d Jun 28 '58
Eliza Bassett Stillman - bp Feb 11 '53, dis Sep '67
Mary Green - bp Feb 11 '53
Aurelia Crandall - bp Feb 11 '53, dis Jan 6 '72

Ellen Crandall - bp Feb 11 '53
Philena Crandall - bp Feb 11 '53
Aurelia Bloss - bp Feb 26 '53, d Feb 1 '54
Clarissa Crandall - bp Feb 26 '53, dis Aug '69
Marcella Crandall - bp Feb 26 '53
Mrs. Katharine Clark - bp Feb 26 '53

CRR 19x57.1   vault
Independence SDB Records
1845-1872   IMS:1995

Ed. notes: 1. First pastorate in conjunction with Andover for Rev. Don A. Sanford.
2. The original clerk did not add the *e* to most of the Clarke and Greene names. A later historian corrected this misspelling. Some of the people still living in the valley still use the Clarke and Greene spellings which originated in RI.

Troupsburg SDB Church 1824-ca 1856
Troupsburg, Steuben Co. NY

No primary records extant

1824: organized by First Alfred at home of Pastor Charles Card
1842: became branch of Independence

List of members

Charles Card
Mrs. C. Card
J. D. Bennet
Mrs. J. D. Bennet
Erastus H. Fisk
George W. Page
Simeon H. Fisk

CRR 19x.57.1   vault
Independence SDB Records
1845-1872   IMS:1995

Hornellsville SDB Church 1877-1914
Hornell, Steuben Co. NY
Located on West Genesee St. near Kanakadea Creek.
It was cleared to become a highway in 1917.

Constituent Members

Rev. T. R. Williams (Never a member here)
Mrs. T. R. Williams
Hiram Pettibone
Dea. O. G. Stillman
Mrs. O. G. Stillman
Alice Swaim
Dea. A. B. Woodward
Mrs. A. B. Woodward
Walter M. Wilbur
Mrs. N. O. Stillman
Mrs. J.E.B. Santee
Jennie Pettibone
Charles Maxson
William Roan
Charles A. Stillman
Stella Pettibone
Mark Satterlee
Nancy Becker

Trustees at incorporation in 1896
Mrs. J. E. B. Santee
Dr. W. E. Palmer
William Hood

From the Notebooks of C. H. Greene
Hornellsville Files: B-File

Pastors
T. R. Williams 1879-80
Byron E. Fisk 1881-82
D. E. Maxson 1883
T. R. Williams 1884
L. A. Platts 1885-89
J. T. Davis 1890-93
George B. Shaw 1894
M. B. Kelly 1895-98
I. L. Cottrell 1899-1902
A. E. Main 1903-05
H. Eugene Davis 1906-07
W. D. Wilcox 1908-1911

Deacons
O. G. Stillman 1879-97
C. A. Stillman 1899-1911

Clerks
A. B. Woodward 1879-80
Elias Ayars 1881
C. A. Stillman 1882-84
J. N. Forbes 1885
W. E. Palmer 1886-92
C. A. Stillman 1893-95
William Hood 1896-1911

From statistics tables in SDB Yearbooks 1879-1914

SDB Mite Society 1882
Hornellsville SDB Church
Hornell, Steuben Co. NY

Membership Roll
Mrs. A. B. Woodward
Mrs. A. Swaim
Mrs. O. G. Stillman
Mrs. C. Maxson
Mrs. J. E. B. Santee
Mrs. E. C. Ayars

Mr. O. G. Stillman
Mr. E. C. Ayars
Mr. A. Swaim
Mr. A. B. Woodward
C. A. Stillman
W. P. Birmingham
Mr. Frank Green
Mrs. Frank Green

Mr. Palmer
Mrs. Palmer
Mr. Jessy Burdick
Iva Palmer
Mr. J. E. B. Santee
Mrs. Shopbelt
Dr. Maxson

CRR x.55 Vault
Hornellsville SDB Church Mite Society 1882-1890

II. CENTRAL ALLEGANY COUNTY SDB CHURCHES

Angelica SDB Society
Phillipsburg Settlement
Angelica, Allegany Co. NY

1816: branch of First Alfred; 1834: united with Amity
no primary records extant

Constituent Members
Theodaty Bliven
Jesse Rogers
Frances Davis
Hannah Rogers
Esther Bliven

Members
Joseph Goodrich - Jun 22 '17
William Davis - Aug 15 '17
James Weed - Nov 20 '18
Davis Stillman - Aug 16 '16
Daniel Bliven
Bethinia Bliven - Aug 15 '17
Barbary Bliven - Aug 15 '17
Abigail Cartwright - Nov 20 '18
Susannah Weed - Nov 20 '18
Fanny Coon - Nov 20 '18
Nancy Rogers - Nov 20 '18
Charlotty Stillman - Nov 20 '18
Abigail Cartwright 2nd
Sarah Stillman
Lydia Harris
Pleates Clark

SDB Society in Angelica
Phillipsburgh Settlement Jul 28, 1816
Scio files: B-file
copied from original by C. H. Greene   IMS:1995

Amity SDB Church 1834-1885 (merged with Scio)
2 miles north of Scio village

Constituent Members
James Weed
John Maxson
Jesse B. Cartwright
Theodaty Bliven
Jesse Rogers
Davis Stillman - d Oct 19 '60
Daniel B. Stillman
William Millard
Ethan Rogers
John C. Cartwright
Theodaty Bliven Jr
Silas C. Bliven
Judeth Lester
Hannah Rogers
Susannah Weed
Nancy Stillman
Hannah Burdick
Rachal Cartwright
Ruth Maxson
Sarah Stillman
Ann Stillman
Elizabeth Millard
Philarman Green
Lydia Green

Members
Phineas Rogers
Hannah Bliven
Buel Oviatt
Lucy Rogers
Prentice Coon
Fanny Oviatt

From the Notebook of C. H. Greene
Scio files: B-file
IMS:1995

Scio SDB Church 1834-1929
also called Willing
Willing Township, Wellsville, Allegany Co. NY

Members

Jesse Rowley
Justus Steely
Nathan Rowley
John D. Greene
Achsa Fish
William Davis
Jonathan Fish
Stephen Tanner
Mary Rowley
Elizabeth Flint Amadown
Amos L. Maxson
Joseph Flint
Jos. Flint Jr
Sally Straight

From the Notebooks of C. H. Greene
Scio files: B-file   IMS:1995
Seventh Day Baptists in Europe and America
Seventh Day Baptist General Conference 1910
Vols. I, II   p. 352, 736, 737

Scio SDB Church Records
Members 1886

p. 3

Mrs. Betsey Young - d May 1 '92
Mrs. Lois Benjamin - d 1906
J. S. Flint - d 1910
Mrs. Susan Smith - d 1891
Mrs. Caroline S. Bliven - d Nov 11 '93
Mrs. Mary U. Smith - d Nov 21 '92
Mrs. J. M. Witter
Henry Striker - d 1900
A. E. Rogers - d Feb 18, 1927
Mrs. Maranda Flint - ad 1876, d '99
Emerson Cartwright - ad 1876, d Aug 3, 1905
Frank Striker - ad 1876
Frank Smith - ad 1876
Mrs. Addie Young - ad 1876, d Jan 18, 1930
Gertrude Smith - ad 1876, dis
A. A. Place - ad 1879, Apr 3 '97
Mrs. Mary E. Rogers - ad 1879, d Jun 15, 1936
Mrs. Hannah J. Hull - ad 1880, d Aug 8, 1910
Thomas W. Sage - ad 1882, dis
Mrs. Abigail Sage - ad 1882, dis
Mrs. Ruth Place - ad 1882, d Apr '95
Mrs. Lorena Canfield - ad 1884, d Oct 23 '98
Lewis C. Canfield - ad 1884, d Feb 29, 1905
Addie Hull Ockerman - ad 1884, d Feb 29, 1904
Charles Stillman - dis

Mrs. Jennie P. Stillman - ad 1884, dis May '90
Mrs. Ida Hull - ad 1884, d Jan 17, 1931
Eva Canfield - ad 1884, dis 1894
Frank Canfield - ad 1886, dis Oct '90
Susie Witter - 1886
Lizzie Flint - ad 1886, d Feb 2, 1925
Minnie Witter - ad 1886, d
Mrs. F. Eva Canfield - ad 1886, dis 1898
John Canfield - ad 1886, dis Mar 8, 1902
Artie Place - ad 1887
Louisa A. Canfield - 1887, dis Jul 18 '96

p. 4

John M. Mosher - ad 1888, dis Jun '90
Flora I. M. Mosher - 1888, dis Jun '90
Jane A. Howe - ad 1889, d
Alfred L. Benjamin - ad 1888
Mrs. Ehma Snyder Roberts - ad 1894; joined
    Adventist Church at Wellsville
Maude Rogers - ad 1898
Rubie Rogers - ad 1898
Lennie Rogers - ad 1898
Cora Young Cartwright - ad 1898, dis Dec 2. 1917
Myrtle Hull - ad 1898, dis
Marcelia Smith - ad 1898, d
Squire Smith - ad 1898, d Jun 11, 1914

CRR 1957.1.2
Scio NY Seventh Day Baptist Church Records
1886-1929
IMS:1995

Wellsville SDB Church (Willing) 1885-1911
Wellsville, Allegany Co. NY
1925-1935: reentered in year book as meeting at Petrolia

Membership

p. 13
1. J. W. Coller - ad Sep 9 '85
2. Ardo Ette G. Coller - ad Sep 9 '85, dis 1919, d
3. Prudence Smith - ad Sep 9 '85, dis Dec 2 '93
4. N. B. Marion - ad Sep 9 '85, d
5. E. S. Miller - ad Sep 9 '85, d
6. Eliza Rowley - ad Sep 9 '85, dis May 27 '88, d
7. Mrs. Ida M. Irish - ad Sep 9 '85, joined Nile
8. Ira S. Crandall - ad Sep 9 '85, d
9. Mrs. Mary E. Almy - ad Sep 9 '85, dis Jan '87
10. Mrs. Hattie E. Goodliff - ad Sep 9 '85, d
11. Mrs. Waity A. Witter - Sep 9 '85
12. Simeon B. Smith - ad Sep 9 '85, dis May '97, d
13. Minerva E. Smith - ad Sep 9 '85, dis Feb '87, d
14. Della M. Sullivan - ad Sep 9 '85, dis Jul 10 '86, dis Jul 21 '94
15. A. W. Sullivan - ad Sep 9 '85, dis Jul 10 '86, ad - Jan 7 '90, dis Jul 21 '94
16. Joshua Green - ad Sep 9 '85, ad Jun 7 '90, dis Nov 24, 1925 d
17. Sarah C. Green - ad Sep 9 '85, dis Feb 22, 1907, d
18. Lorenzo Witter - ad by experience Nov '85, d
19. Mrs. Mattie A. Witter - ad Nov 14 '85
20. Mrs. Janette Hallock - bp
21. Henry L. Jones - ad Aug 14 '86, dis Mar 21 '91 ad Aug 11 '94
22. Mrs. Emma Jones - ad Aug 14 '86 dis Mar 28 '91, d
23. Chester D. Mills - ad by experience Jan 1 '87, d
24. Mrs. Deucia Mills - ad by experience Jan 1 '87
25. Alice H. Perkins - ad Mar 5 '87
26. Mrs. Mariah Davis - ad Mar 19 '87, dis '91, d
27. Edgar F. Stelle - ad May 19 '87, dis Jun '91, d
28. Mrs. Elizabeth Packard - ad May 21 '87, dp
29. W. W. Crandall - ad Sep 3 '87, d
30. Mrs. E. E. Crandall - ad Sep 3 '87, d
31. William Lasher - Sep 3 '87, dis Nov. 16 '93
32. Matilda Lasher - ad Sep 3 '87, dis Nov 16 '93
33. Mrs. Fanny Stannard - bp Dec 10 '87, d
34. Genia A. Mills - bp Dec 31 '87

p. 14
35. Elsa S. York - ad by experience Sep 22 '88
36. Ellen A. York - ad Sep 22 '88, d
37. Eusebia Stillman - ad Sep 22 '88
38. John D. Mills - ad by experience Sep 22 '88, d
39. Mrs. Louisa Davidson - ad Oct 27 '88, dp dis Nov. 16 '93
40. Zureal C. Witter - bp Feb 25 '89, dp
41. Glen Davidson - bp Feb 9 '89, dp
42. Blanche Davidson - bp Feb 9 '89, dp
43. Mary E. Lasher - bp Feb 16 '89, dp
44. Josie Witter - bp Feb 16 '89
45. Bettie Mills - bp Feb 16 '89
46. Virgil F. Randolph - ad Feb 23 '89
47. Betsey Knox - ad Mar 16 '89, d
48. William Allen - ad by experience Aug 3 '89, dp
49. Eliza Allen - ad by experience Aug 3 '89, dp
50. Eugene Witter - bp Jan 4 '90
51. Clara Burdick Hotchkiss - bp Jan 4 '90
52. Ora Hallock - bp Jan 4 '90
53. Mrs. Ira S. Crandall - bp Jan 18 '90, d
54. Annie Stedsell West - bp Jan 1 '90, dis May 12 '94
55. Mrs. Mary Ette Elliott - ad Apr 5 '90, dp
56. Samuel Lee Burdick - ad Jul 7 '90, d
    Mr. and Mrs. A. W. Sullivan - ad Jul 7 '90 dis Dec 16 '93
57. L. G. Backus - ad Mar 21 '91, dp
58. Abbie Elster - bp Jul 2 '92
59. Albert W. Crandall - ad Aug 20 '92 dis Nov. 16 '93
60. Hallie E. A. Crandall - ad Aug 20 '92
61. Martie J. Barber - ad Jul 7 '94
62. Mary W. Barber - ad Jul 7 '94
63. Lillie Barber - ad Jul 7 '94
64. Olive Jones - ad May 23 '95, d
65. Milton Loring - bp Mar 22 '95
66. Ada York Loring - Aug '94, d

Residents: No dates
1. J. Wheeler
2. Ardo E. Wheeler - d
3. Esther A. Mills -d
4. Ira S. Crandall -d
5. Mrs. I. S. Crandall -d
6. Waity A. Witter
7. Eugene Witter
8. Joshua Green
9. Sarah C. Green -d
10. Lorenzo Witter -d
11. Mattie A, Witter
12. Josie Witter
13. Janette Hallock
14. Glenna Hallock Crofoot
15. Henry L. Jones -d
16. Olive Jones - d
17. C. D. Mills - d
18. Denise Mills
19. Genie Mills
20. W. W. Crandall - d
21. E. E. Crandall - d
22. Elsie S. York - never come
23. Ellen A. York - never come, d
24. none
25. Eusebia Stillman - never come, d
26. Virgil F. Randolph
27. William Allen - d
28. Martin V. Barber - moved
29. Wany W. Barber - moved
30. Lillie Barber - moved
31. Milton Loring
32. Ada York Loring - d
33. Lena Miller
34. Cash Miller

p. 15 Non Residents
1. Ida M. Irish
2. Hattie E. Goodliff -d
3. Louisa Davidson - joined Adventist Church at Jamestown
4. Blanche Davidson - joined Adventist Church at Jamestown
5. Glenn Davidson - joined Adventist Church at Jamestown
6. Bettie Mills
7. Betsey Knox - d
8. Clara Burdick Hotchkiss
9. L. G. Backus
10. Abbie Elston
11. Alice Perkins Mistoe

CRR 19x.203 vault
Wellsville NY SDB church records, 1885-1911
IMS:1995

Scio Branch SDB Church 1871-1882

Knight's Creek, Willing Township, Allegany Co NY
Follow up of Scio which was also called Willing
Located where Allentown NY now stands

Members

Dillen Lewis
Martin Emerson
S.B Smith
B. J. Emerson
William Allen
Sarah Phillips

Polly Emerson
Adelaide Williams
Lavina Kenyon
Mariah Clark
Betsey Emerson
Eliza Allen

Old Manuscript by Rev. H.N. Jordan of Scio

Seventh Day Baptists in Europe and America
**Seventh Day Baptist General Conference 1910
Vols. I, II   p. 736, 745, 768   IMS:1995**

Stannard's Corners SDB Church 1875-1880
**Stannard's Corners, Willing Township, Allegany Co. NY
First called Willing, offshoot of Scio**

Members

S. M. Cottrell
John D. Mills
Luke G. Witter
Ruth J. Witter
D. P. Witter
Betsey Witter
Lorenzo Witter
Mattie S. Witter - fr 1st Alfred

Chester D. Mills - bp 1884
Densie Mills - bp 1884
Franklin M. Witter - bp 1884
Libbie S. Witter - bp 1884
Hellen Witter - bp 1884
William Snow - ad 1881, rj 1877
Elsa York - ad 1881
Ellen York - ad 1881 fr 1st Alfred

**Original Church Record Book of Church Clerk Lorenzo Witter
Willing-Stannard's Corners files: B file**

Seventh Day Baptists in Europe and America
**Seventh Day Baptist General Conference 1910
Vols. I, II p. 736, 768   IMS:1995**

Friendship SDB Church 1824-ca 1830, 1834-1959
Nile, Allegany Co. NY
First record book not extant;
2 compilations based on it follow:

Friendship Membership Record 1824-1879
transcribed from old record book in 1839

Constituent Members

p. 1

Abraham C. Crandall - ad 1824, d Jan 23 '70
Samuel Yapp - ad 1824, dis 1851
Mary Yapp w/o Samuel - ad 1824, dis 1851
Nathan Gruman - ad 1824, dis 1835
Cary Crandall - ad 1824, d May 25 '44
Mahitable Crandall w/o Cary - ad 1824, d Apr '54

Benjamin Wigden (colored) - ad 1824, d 1828
Mary Wigden (colored) w/o Benjamin - ad 1824 dis 1836
Micah F. Randolph - ad 1824, d 1837
Anna Randolph w/o Micah - ad 1824, dis 1834
Elizabeth Noble - ad 1824, d Jan 19 '65
Henry R. Green - ad 1824, dis 1827
Edith Ayars - ad 1824, d 1831

Members

p. 2

Roxana Messenger - probably ad 1826, joined Richburg
James A. Dunham - ad 1826, dis 1837
Elder John Green - ad 1826, dis 1831
Elizabeth Green w/o John - ad 1826, dis 1831
Catherine Allen - ad 1826, dis 1847
Squire Dunn - ad 1826, dis 1851
Joel Kenyon - ad 1826, dis 1835
Lavinna Kenyon w/o Joel - ad 1826, dis 1834
Harvey Stannard - ad 1826, d Nov 4, 187_
Nancy Stannard - ad 1826, d 1826
Ezekiel Johnson - ad 1826, d spring 1852
Rowland G. Green - ad 1826, dis 1846
Joanna Green w/o Rowland - ad 1826, dis 1846
Richard B. Davis - ad 1826, dis 1857
Mary Davis w/o Richard - ad 1826, d 1827
Z_____ Ayars - ad 1826, dis 1830
Rachel Ayars w/o Z_____ - ad 1826, dis 1830
Josiah D. Ayars - ad 1826, d May 12, _____
John Covey - ad 1826, ex 1839
Margaret Covey w/o John - ad 1826, dis 1851
Daniel Willard - ad 1826, ex 1834
Henry Smalley - ad 1826, dis 1834
Noah Smalley w/o Henry - ad 1826, ex 1830
Mary Ann Smalley - ad 1827, dis 1857
Samuel Crandall - ad 1827
Anna Crandall w/o Henry - ad 1827, d Mar 186__
Henry Smalley Jr - ad 1827, dis 1854
Chillen Smalley w/o Henry - ad 1827, ex 1836
Charlotte Smalley - ad 1827, d

Abel Maxson - ad 1827, dis
George Ayars - ad 1827, dis 1834
Sarah Ayars w/o George - ad 1827, dis 1834
Samuel B. Ayars - ad 1827, dis 1834
Rev. Walter B. Gillette - ad 1827, dis 1840
Sarah Ann Gillette, ad 1827, dis 1840
Fanny Hull - ad 1827, ex 1837

p. 3

Augustus Kenyon - ad 1827, dis 1834
Joanna Kenyon w/o Augustus Kenyon - ad 1827, d 1830
John M. Mills - ad 1827, dis 1837
Lydia Mills w/o John - ad 1827, dis 1837
Sally Dunham - ad 1827, dis 1837
Joseph C. Green - ad 1827
Abigail Green - ad 1827, dis 1851
Elizabeth Yapp - ad 1828, d
Azariah A. A. F. Randolph - ad 1828, dis 1857
Lucy C. Randolph w/o Azariah - ad 1828, dis 1857
John Ayars - ad 1824, d 1834
Phebe Smalley - ad 1824, dis 1834
Benjamin Wigden Jr (colored) - ad 1824, d 1825
Lydia Davidson - ad 1825, d 1828
Permelia Phillips - ad 1825, dis 1837
James Maxson - ad 1825, d 1866
Lucinda Maxson - ad 1825, d Jul __, 1841
Lemuel Thogens - ad 1826, dis
Salina Gruman - ad 1826, dis
Phebe Ayars - ad 1828, d 1851
Experience Dunn - ad 1828, dis 1857
Elizabeth Willard - ad 1828, ex 1834

Sarah Lenox - ad 1828, ex 1832
Rogers Crandall - ad 1828, dis 1851
Josiah Wheeler - ad 1828, d 1833
Eunice Wheeler w/o Josiah - ad 1828, d Feb '68
Alonson Kenyon - ad 1828, dis 1834
Thomas C. Williams - ad 1829, ex 1835
Renewet Williams w/o Thomas - ad 1829 dis 1851
Salenina Gruman - ad 1829, dis 1851
Lucy Stannard - ad 1829, d 1831
Eunice Alott - ad 1829, dis 1834
Lois Smalley - ad 1829, dis 1851
Mary Parcell - ad 1829, dis 1833
Berthany Widgen (colored) - ad 1829, dis 1836
Judsen Dacon - ad 1829, dis 1834
Ezekiel Huff - ad 1829, excom Sep 16 '60
Mary Huff (colored) - ad 1829, d Apr '67
Dea. Alain Ayars - ad 1830, dis 1857
Eadith Ayars w/o Alain - ad 1830, dis 1857
Amos L. Maxson - ad 1830, dis 1835
Ambrose Coats - ad 1830, dis 1834
_____ Coats w/o Ambrose - ad 1830, dis 1834

p. 4

Louisa Stannard - ad 1830, d
Polly Maxson - ad 1830, dis 1837
Eliza Maxson - ad 1830, dis 1857
Fanny Smalley - ad 1830, dis 1851
Martha Johnson - ad 1830, dis
Mary Rino - ad 1830, dis 1834
Sally Stuck - ad 1831, ex 1832
Jacob Dacon - ad 1831, dis 1834
Mahalan Dacon w/o Jacob - ad 1831, dis 1834
James Hyett - ad 1831, ex 1836
Martha Hyett w/o James - ad 1831, dis 1857
Ezekiel Johnson - ad 1831, excom Jul 12, 1874
Deideamia D. W. Green - ad 1831, dis 1857
Samantha Maxson - ad 1831, ex 1846
Eunice Holtlin - ad 1832, dis 1857
Rhoda Wilcox - ad 1832, d 1833
Marvel Wilcox, 1832, dis 1834
Polly Maxson - ad 1832, dis 1835
Aley Johnson - ad 1832, d 1878
Sally Cole - ad 1832, dis 1857
Clarinda S. Gruman - ad 1832, dis
Rebecca Smalley - ad 1832, dis 1851
Orlando Holcomb - ad 1832, dis 1857
Asenith Holcomb w/o Orlando - ad 1833, dis
Eunice Colegrove - ad 1833, d Feb 14 '72
Oliver H. P. Cole - ad 1833, dis 1851
Harriet Hudson - ad 1833, dis 1851
Alonzo A. Coon - ad 1833, dis 1857
Zacheus Morton - ad 1833, dis 1834
Sally Morton w/o Zacheus - ad 1833, dis 1834
Jonathan D. Ayars - ad 1833, ex 1834
Hannah Ayars w/o Jonathan - ad 1833, ex 1834
Anna Cotten - ad 1833, d Mar 1869
Sally Foster Wilcox - ad 1833, ex 1835
Elias Rogers - ad 1833, dis 1839
Content Rogers w/o Elias - ad 1833, dis 1839
Daniel Crandall - ad 1833, d 1835

p. 5

Robert Allen - ad 1833, d 1836
Mary Dacon - ad 1833, dis 1834
Lunna Crandall - ad 1833, d Jul '52
Anna Stannard - ad 1833, d
Nancy Clark - ad 1833, d Jun 17, ____
Rhoda McLaferday - ad 1833, ex 1833
Gracy Kenyon - ad 1833, d 1837
Eleanor Maxson - ad 1833, dis 1834
John R. Randolph - ad 1833, dis 1834
Albert F. Randolph - ad 1833, excom 1839
Ansel Stannard - ad 1833
Enoch A. Crandall - ad 1833, ex 1857
Jonathan D. Ayars - ad 1833, dis
Elias Smalley - ad 1833, dis
David Smalley - ad 1833, ex 1833
Enos Crandall - ad 1833
Mathew W. Green - ad 1833, dis 1846
Nathan Green - ad 1833, dis 1857
Aden Stannard - ad 1833, dis 1857
Heziah Noble - ad 1833, d
Fanny W. Green - ad 1833, dis 1832
Elizabeth L. Green - ad 1833, dis 1832
Saloma Covey - ad 1833, ex 1837
Ersula Wilcox - ad 1833
Samuel Allen - ad 1833, ex 1850, rest Sep 3 '76, dis Oct 12 '76
Amy Allen w/o Samuel - ad 1833, d 1846
John Maxson - ad 1833, dis 1834
Job Maxson - ad 1833, dis 1832
Sheffield W. Green - ad 1833, excom
Joseph Maxson - ad 1833, dis 1832
David Maxson - ad 1833, dis 1833
James Maxson 2nd - ad 1833, ex 1835
Elisha C. Green - ad 1833, dis
Ezekiel Clark - ad 1833
Moses Maxson - ad 1833, dis 1833
Nancy Maxson - ad 1833, dis 1833

p. 6

Cyrus Cotten - ad 1833, ex 1848
Jared Stannard - ad 1833, ex 1838
Isaac A. Crandall - ad 1833, ex 1835
Lucina Crandall - ad 1833, dis 1857
Horatio Yapp - ad 1834, ex 1843
Francis Mills - ad 1834, dis 1837
Ellen Cotten - ad 1834, dis Aug 1864
Harriet Maxson - ad 1834, dis 1857
Ezra Luther - ad 1834, dis 1857
Joseph Allen - ad 1834

Phebe Allen w/o Joseph - ad 1834
Mary Weatherby - ad 1834, dis 1857
Jane Smalley - ad 1834, dis 1857
Phoebe Smalley - ad 1834, dis 1857
Clarinda Gruman - ad 1834, dis 1857
Ann Hand - ad 1834, dis 1857
Lacy Green - ad 1834, dis 1835
Mary A. Coats - ad 1835, dis 1836
Ray Coats - ad 1835, dis
Maxson Johnson - ad 1835, d Feb 25, ____
Sally Green - ad 1835, dis 1846
Jacob Ayars - ad 1835, dis 1837
Alpheus M. Green - ad 1835, dis
Abby L. Green - ad 1836, dis 1857
Jonathan Coon - ad 1836, dis 1857
Martha Coon - ad 1836, dis 1857
Juliette Cotton - ad 1836, d. Oct 19 '71
Phebe Green - ad 1836, dis 8157
Peter Burdick - ad 1836
John L. Thurston - ad 1836, d Dec 5, 185_
Nathan Truman - ad 1837, dis
Deborah A. Cotten - ad 1837, d Oct 1, '65

p. 7

Squire P. Witter - ad 1837, excom 1872
Mary A. Witter w/o Squire - ad 1837
John Gruman - ad 1837, dis 1857
Mariah Gruman w/o John - ad 1837, dis 1857
Anna Davis - ad 1837, dis 1857
Betsey Vars - ad 1837
Mariah N. Vanvelsor - ad 1838, excom 1859
Lucy A. Green - ad 1838, dis 1851
Azus L. Burdick w/o William - ad 1838
William Burdick Jr - ad 1838
Nancy Thurston - ad 1838, d 1847
James L. Scott - ad 1838, dis
Daniel Potter - ad 1838, dis 1848
Rebecca Potter w/o Daniel - ad 1838, dis 1848
Elias Wells - ad 1838, dis Apr 21, '44
Eveline Wells w/o Elias - ad 1838
   dis Apr 21 '44
William Gruman - ad 1838, d Dec 8 '42
Elder Zurial Campbell - ad 1840, dis 1845
Amy Campbell - ad 1840, dis 1845
Thomas Clarke - ad 1840, excom May 7 '54
Diana Clarke w/o Thomas - ad 1840,
   excom May 7 '54
John Maxson - ad 1840, dis 1857
Anna Crandall - ad 1840, d May 1845
Ambrose Coats - ad 1840, d
Mary Coats w/o Ambrose - ad 1840, d

Randall Ryno - ad 1841, dis
Maryann Ryno w/o Randolph - ad 1841, dis
Olivar G. Perry - ad 1841, d Jul 6 '41 1851
Rebecca T. Perry w/o w/o Olivar - ad 1841, dis
Almeron P. Stillman - ad 1841
Hannah Stillman - ad 1841, d Jun 23 '43
Lovina Stillman - ad 1841, dis
Phebe Wheeler - ad 1841

p. 8

Mathew Stillman - ad 1842, d
Amanda Stillman w/o Mathew - ad 1842, dis 1857
James Brown - ad 1842, dis 1846
Titus I. Giddings - ad 1842, dis
Jane Giddings w/o Titus - ad 1842, dis
Jesse W. Johnson - ad 1842, d Feb 23, 184_
Dennis M. Johnson - ad 1842, dis
Stillman G. Greene - ad 1842, dis 1846
Sophia Crandall w/o Enos P. - ad 1843
Flavina Giddings - ad 1843, dis 1951
Sivena Spicer - ad 1843, excom Sep 184_
Cynthia S. Truman - ad 1843, dis 1857
George Day - ad 1843, excom Sep 3, 184_
Henry H. Johnson - ad 1843, dis Dec 183_
John T. Vars - ad 1843, dis
John Greene - ad 1843, dis 1846
Courtland L. Johnson - ad 1843, excom
Albert H. Truman - ad 1843, dis
Mercy Greene - ad 1843, dis 1846
Anna S. Truman - ad 1843, dis
Sarah Ann Enos Rogers - ad 1843, dis
Achsa Truman - ad 1843, dis
Alonzo Truman - ad 1843, dis
Juliane M. Wells - ad 1843, dis
Abigail A. Wells - ad 1843, dis
Almira Crandall Gardiner - ad 1843
Rosena Crandall - ad 1843
Amarilla Maxson - ad 1843, d
Abel S. Maxson - ad 1843, dis
George W. Maxson - ad 1843, dis
Abigail Ann Maxson - ad 1843, dis
Welthy Brown - ad 1843
Charles Witter - ad 1843, d Andersonville
George Witter - ad 1843, excom

p. 9

Samuel Hurd - ad 1843, d
Menerva Hurd w/o Samuel - ad 1843, d
Emeline Fisk - ad 1844, dis
Squire B. Strong - ad 1844, d
Rebecca Hubbard - ad 1845
Ethan Lanphere - ad 1846, excom
Lois Lanphere - ad 1846, d

Daniel Potter - ad 1846, dis
Rebecca Potter w/o Daniel - ad 1846, dis
Eunice Babcock - ad 1846, d
Ezra Crandall - ad 1846, dis 1869
Mary Crandall w/o Ezra - ad 1846, dis 1869
Horrace Giddings - ad 1846, dis
Sarah Ann Willcox - ad 1846, dis 1867
Ann Maxson - ad 1846
Marion Crandall - ad 1846, dis
Hannah T. Stannard - ad 1845, joined Milton
Joel Kenyon - ad 1846, d Jan 20 '78
Braton Babcock - ad 1846
Reuben W. Utter - ad 1846, d May 1853
Mary E. Utter w/o Reuben - ad 1846, dis
Jennette Clarke - ad 1846, d Mar 1864
Emory Lanphere - ad 1846, d 1847
Hannah B. Johnson - ad 1846, excom Jul 12 '71
Phymando Willcox - ad 1846, d Jun 4 '54
Rhoda Hubbard - ad 1846, excom Jun 12, 185_
Rev. B. F. Robbins - ad 1848, excom
Mary Ann Robbins w/o B. F. - ad 1848, excom
Harriet W. Clarke - bp 1850, dis
Louisa Morris - ad 1850, excom
Mary Ann Johnson - ad 1850, d Jun 11 '56
Sally Brown - ad 1850, d spring '52
Lavinia Coats - bp 1850
Mrs. Mary Babcock - ad 1850, dis
Mrs. Angeline Clarke - ad 1850, dis

p. 10

Helen E. Clarke - bp 1850, dis
Harriott Maudane Clarke - bp 1850, dis
Martin W. Babcock - ad 1850, dis
Joanna Kenyon - bp 1850
Avery Lanphere - ad 1851, excom
Caroline Johnson - bp 1852, dis
Euphemia Allen - bp 1852, dis
Caroline Ayars - bp 1852, dis
Deloss Crandall - bp 1853, dis
Zelora E. Brown - bp 1853, excom
Sarah A. Brown - bp 1853
Huldah Lanphere - bp 1853, excom
Lavinnia P. Lanphere - bp 1853
Caroline D. Babcock - bp 1853, dis 1857
Amelia Finett Clarke - bp 1853, d
Noah R. Brown - bp 1853, excom
Samuel A. Yapp - bp 1853, d
Hannah A. Witter - bp 1853
Sally Maria Witter - bp 1853, d
Mary C. Witter - bp 1853, d
Eliza Culver - bp 1853, excom
Elisha Hyde - bp 1853
Daniel J. Brown - bp 1853, excom

Sarah Babcock - bp 1853, d
Salina T. Johnson - bp 1853, dis
Paulina A. Johnson - bp 1853, dis
William Wightman - bp 1853
Emelia Wightman - bp 1853
Antinett Enos - bp 1853, dis
Lewis H. Kenyon - bp 1853
Mary C. Yapp - bp 1853, excom
Hamit Stannard - bp 1853, excom
Almira M. Allen - bp 1853, dis
Edna H. Clarke - ad 1853, d

p. 11

Nathan Truman - ad 1854, d Apr 1871
Roxy Truman w/o Nathan - ad 1854, dis 1876
Bailer Curtis - ad 1854, d Aug 4, 1856
Prudence Coon - ad 1855
Martha N. Burdick - bp 1856
Judith Hyde - bp 1856, d Feb 11, 1860
Hamit Lanphere - bp 1857, dis May 1867
Joel C. West - ad 1857, dis 1865
Malvina E. West - ad 1857, dis 1864
Joel G. Saunders - ad 1850, exco 1860
Martha S. Saunders - ad 1858, excom 1860
Daniel E. Babcock - bp 1858, excom 1874
Franklin G. Clarke - bp 1858, excom 1864
Orson Witter - bp 1858
Alvin A. Place - ad 1858, excom 1874
Ruth A. Place - ad 1858
Rosalia V. Green - ad 1858, dis
Samuel Eugene Burdick - bp 1858, d Apr 30 '59
Alpheus Vars - bp 1858, d by drowning
    Spring 18__
Ethan Lanphere - ad 1858, dis, rest
Hannah Lanphere - ad 1859, d 1878
Sarah Spicer - ad 1859 from Methodist Church
Charles Sisson - ad 1859
Thankful Childs - ad 1860, dis 1867
George B. Tanner - ad 1860, d Andersonville
    Jun 17 '64
Hamit Tanner w/o George - ad 1860
Dennis Johnson - ad 1860
Selina T. Johnson w/o Dennis - ad 1860
Abbey K. Witter - ad 1860, dis
William D. Crandall - ad 1860
Califurnia Crandall w/o William - ad 1860
Alonzo Coon - ad 1860, d Aug 25, 1887
Abby Coon w/o Alonzo - ad 1860, d Oct 25 '72
Cornelia Coon - ad 1860

p. 12

David C. Gardiner - ad 1860
Floretta Gardiner w/o David - ad 1860
Lucy B. Jacobs - bp 1860, dis

Sarah M. Ayars Eldridge - bp 1861, excom
Henrietta L. Enos Burdick - bp 1861
Emily I. Place Gardiner - bp 1861, dis
Emma M. Coon Witter - bp 1861, dis
Hellen M. Jacobs - bp 1862, dis
Laura M. Crandall - bp 1862
Susan A. Wheeler - bp 1862, excom
Oscar Kenyon - ad 1862, dis
Horace D. Witter - bp 1862
Mary M. Rogers - bp 1862, ex (?)
Lydia Ann Strong - bp 1862
Rev. Leman Andrus - ad 1863, dis
Caroline Hawley - ad 1863, dis
Rosalia Kenyon - bp 1863
Dorcas Vars - ad 1864
Welthy Ann Andrus - ad 1864, dis
Ellis Adelbert Witter - bp 1865, dp
Paul B. Clarke - bp 1866, dis
Lucy E. Clarke - bp 1866, dis
Jennie M. Hubbard - bp 1866, excom
Jennie A. Place - bp 1866, dis
Allis Z. Coon Fleming - ad 1866, d Dec 1924
Mary G. Strong - bp 1866, excom
Frances A. Spicer - bp 1866, dis
Nellie E. Maxson - bp 1866
W. Marcus Wightman - bp 1866, d May 31, 1924
Chester S. Clarke - bp 1866, dis
Theodore L. Gardiner - bp 1866, dis
Sarah Gardiner - bp 1866, dis
Harman D. Johnson - bp 1866
Levi C. Strong - bp 1866, dis 1867
M. H. Elvine Crandall - bp 1866, dis

p. 13
Elnora A. Gardner - bp 1866, dis
Ardiutt Gardner - bp 1866
L. Estella Crandall - bp 1866, d
Mary L. Wright - ad 1866
Hannah C. Clarke - ad 1866
Edmond S. Clarke - bp 1866
Olive Morley Davis - bp 1866
Almira A. Witter - bp 1866
H. Francelia Witter - bp 1866
Louise Gardner - bp 1866, dis May 5 '78
Arloene Clarke - bp 1866, dis
Rev. L. A. Platts - ad 1866, dis Sep 1 '68
Emma A. F. Platts w/o L.A. - ad 1866
    dis Sep 1'68
Polly B. Clarke - ad 1866, d Jul 20'69
Sarah A. Rogers - ad 1866, excom, d Feb 14 '86
William W. Gardner - ad 1868

Mary Peckham - ad 1866
Eliza A. Witter - ad 1867
Ida M. Wightnan - bp 1868
Edna E. Wightman - bp 1868, dis
Ida A. Tanner - bp 1868
Amanda M. Loveland - bp 1868
Samuel T. Burdick - bp 1868, d Mar 1, 1915
William H. Rogers - bp 1868
Frederick S. Pace - bp 1868, dis Jan 1 '77
Amanda M. Burdick - bp 1868, d Jan 31, 1924
F. Adecen Witter - bp 1868
A. Leona Babcock - bp 1868
Mary Wheeler - bp 1868
Myrta Gardener - bp 1868
Elden Crandall - bp 1868
Willet Burdick - bp 1868
Sarah A. Clarke - ad 1868
Jennie Witter - bp 1868
Juliette Babcock - bp 1868, d
J. L. Huffman - ad 1868, dis

p. 14
Samuel P. Crandall Jr - ad 1870
Marion Crandall w/o Samuel - ad 1870
Almira W. Hamilton - ad 1870
Jesse O. Hamilton - bp 1870
Julia E. Allen - bp 1870
Alonzo G. Crofoot - bp 1870, dis
Mary Matilda Compton - bp 1870
Lauraett Compton - bp 1870
George W. Burdick - bp 1870
Charles C. Clarke - bp 1870
Eva G. Gardner - bp 1870
Albert C. Rogers - bp 1870
Herbert H. Gardner - bp 1870, dis
Sarah E. Clarke - bp 1870
Eva V. German - bp 1870, dis Mar 26 '71
Francis M. Kenyon - bp 1870
George R. Babcock - bp 1870
Mary Alice Crandall - bp 1870
Mary Z. German - bp 1870
Myron C. Irish - bp 1870
Winslow Lathrop - bp 1871
Frank Hassard - bp 1871, excom
Ettie E. Dutcher - ad 1871, dis
Charles M. Mix - ad 1871
Benjamin F. Rogers - ad 1871, dis
Adeline M. Rogers - ad 1871, dis
Henry D. Green - bp 1872
Sarah C. Green - bp 1872

John Fuller - bp 1872
John Crandall - ad 1872
Eliza Crandall - ad 1872
Chester S. Clarke - bp 1872
Ophelia A. Clarke - ad 1871
Anna L. Rogers - bp 1877
Angie Clarke - bp 1877
Milton J. Jordan - bp 1877
Charles Gardener - bp 1877
Lina Jordan - bp 1877
Mabel Witter - bp 1877
Samuel Orlie Willard - bp 1877
Daniel Evert Willard - bp 1877
Evelyn Adell Willard - bp 1877
Mrs. Mary Lucinda Burdick - bp 1878
Mary Emmogen Babcock - bp 1878

p. 15
Edgar L. Vincent - bp 1873
Sarah E. Sisson - bp 1873
Henrietta I. Rogers - bp 1873
Arlie Tanner - bp 1873
Rev. W. B. Gillette - ad 1876
Mrs. W. B. Gillette - ad 1876
William Hyde - bp 1877
Eugene Hyde - bp 1877
Susie E. Clarke - bp 1877
Delette Gardner - bp 1877
Will Crandall - bp 1877
Carrie E. Rogers - bp 1877
Maud Clarke - bp 1877
Elbert R. Smith - bp 1878
Clarrissa Edwards - ad 1878

p. 16
Ephraim Allison Curtis - bp 1879
Mrs. Elva Maria Rogers - ad 1879
Jasper W. Coller - bp 1879

CRR 19x.48.1   vault
Fiendship SDB Records 1824-1879
IMS:1995

Friendship Church Register 1830-1956
transcribed from old book in 1879

Membership

p. 1

Ellen Cotten - ad 1834, d Jun '81
Ansel Stannard - ad 1830, d
Enos Crandall - ad 1830, d Dec '98
Ezekel R. Clarke - ad 1830, d Jul '89
Joseph Allen - ad 1834, d Sep '98
Phebe Allen - ad 1834, d Dec 29 '81
Peter Burdick - ad 1836, d Jun '82
Squire P. Witter - ad 1837, ordained deacon Jun 23 '61, d Nov 15 '82
Mary A. Witter - ad 1837, d Jul 22 '97
Betsey Vars Witter - ad 1837, d Jun 9 '83
William Burdick - ad 1838, d Mar '87
Avis L. Burdick - ad 1838, d 1891
Phebe Wheeler - ad 1841, d Jul 22 '97
Sophia Crandall - ad 1843, d Feb 24 '86
Rebecca Hubbard - ad 1845, d 1882
Brayton Babcock - ad 1846, d Mar 8 '87
Joanna Kenyon Maxson - bp 1850, d 1897
Sarah A. Brown Wells - ad 1853, dis 1887
Lavinia Willard - ad 1853, d Apr 1897
Hannah Babcock - ad 1853
Elisha Hyde - ad 1853
Almira Crandall Gardner - ad 1843

p. 2

Hannah R. Johnson - ad 1846, d Mar 25 '83
Caroline Ayers Burdick - bp '52, d May 1900
William Wightman - bp 1852, d
Emelia Wightman - bp 1852
Lewis H. Kenyon - ad 1852, d
S. P. Crandall - ad 1870
Marion Crandall - ad 1870, d May 24 '82
Prudence Coon - ad 1855, d Aug 16 '87
Martha Davidson - bp 1856, d
Orson M. Witter - bp 1858, d
Daniel E. Babcock - bp 1858, ordained deacon Jun 3 '61, d Oct '98
Ruth A. Place - ad 1858, dis
Charles Sisson - ad 1859, d Jun '88
Dennis Johnson - ad 1860, d 1892
Selina Johnson - ad 1860
William D. Crandall - ad 1861, d
Calfernia Crandall - ad 1861, d
Alonzo Coon - ad 1861, d Aug 25 '87
Abby Coon - ad 1861, d Oct 25 '82
David Gardiner - ad 1861, d
Floretta Gardiner - ad 1861, d Aug 1 '93

Sarah M. Ayers - bp 1862, dp Jan 6, 1902
Henrietta Enos Burdick - bp 1862, d
Emma M. Coon Witter - bp 1862
Laura M. Miller - bp 1862, excom May 27 '88
Horace D. Witter - bp 1862
Lydia Ann Strong - ad 1862, d May 20 '87
Rosalia Kenyon Mix - bp 1863, dis
Rosena Crandall Hyde - ad 1843, d 1904
Harriet Tanner - ad 1860, d 1896

p. 3

Alice G. Coon Champhagne Fleming - bp 1866
Nellie E. Maxson - bp 1866, ex Jun 7 '85
W. Marcus Wightman - ad 1866, dp Jan 6, 1902
Ardo Ett Gardiner Coller - ad 1866, dis Aug '85
Mary R. Wright - ad 1866
Hannah Champlain - bp 1866, d
Edmond S. Clarke - bp 1866, dis
Olive Morley Clarke - bp 1866, dis 1900
Almira A. Witter - ad 1866, d Jan 2 '90
H. Francelia Witter Burdick - bp 1866
Sarah Ann Rogers - ad 1867, d Feb 12 '86
Eliza A. Witter - ad 1867, d 1900
William R. Gardiner - ad testimony 1868, ordained deacon Dec 7 '78
Ida Wightman Irish - bp 1868, dis Sep 5 '85
Edna Wightman Green - bp 1868, dis
Ida Tanner Slade - bp 1868, dis May 16 '85
Amanda M. Loveland - bp 1868
William H. Rogers - bp 1868, dis
Samuel T. Burdick - bp 1868
Amanda M. Burdick - bp 1868, d
F. Adene Witter - bp 1868, d Nov '98
A. Leona Babcock Clarke - bp 1868, d Dec 21 '81
Mary E. Wheeler Eaton - bp 1868, excom Sep '94
Mertie Gardiner Rogers - bp 1868, dis
Ellen A. Crandall Irish - bp 1868
Willet Burdick - bp 1868
Sarah A. Clarke - ad 1868, dis Nov '85
Jennie Witter - ad 1868, d 1893

p. 4

Almira W. Hamilton - bp 1870
Jesse O. Hamilton - bp 1870, d 1892
Julia E. Allen - bp 1870
Lanraett Compton - bp 1870, dis
Mary M. Compton - bp 1870, d

George W. Burdick - bp 1870, d
C. Clayton Clarke - bp 1870, dis Jul 7 '99
Eva L. German - bp 1870
Albert C. Rogers - bp 1870
Sarah E. Clarke Greenman - bp 1870, ex Jun '85
Eva G. Gardiner - bp 1870, d '99
Frances M. Kenyon - bp 1870
George P. Babcock - bp 1870, d Jun 10 '81
M. Alice Crandall - bp 1870
Mary J. German - bp 1870, d
Myron C. Irish - bp 1870, d
Winslow Latham - bp 1871
Charles M. Mix - bp 1871, dis
Henry D. Green - bp 1872, d Mar 22, 1905
Sarah C. Green - bp 1872
John Fuller - bp 1872, d Nov 5 '86
John Crandall - bp 1882, ordained deacon Dec 7 '73, d Mar 20 '84
Eliza Crandall - bp 1872
Chester S. Clarke - bp 1872, dis 1899
Ophelia A. Clarke - bp 1872, dis 1899
Edgar L. Vincent - bp 1873, ex Jan 4 '85
Sarah E. Sisson - bp 1873
Henriette J. Rogers - bp 1873

p. 5

Arlie Tanner Stanton - bp 1873, excom Sep 2 '83
Rev. W. B. Gillette, D. D. - ad 1876, dis
Mrs. W. B. Gillette - ad 1876, dis
William D. Hyde - bp 1877, dis, Mar '94
E. Eugene Hyde - bp 1877
Susie E. Clarke Stillman - bp 1877, dis
William Delette Gardiner - bp 1877, dis Jul '93
William C. Crandall - bp 1877, dis Sep '91
C. Ella Rogers - bp 1877, d 1949
Anna L. Rogers - bp 1877, d Apr 21 '84
Maud F. Clarke - bp 1877
Angie Clarke - bp 1877
Milton J. Jordan - bp 1877
Charles Gardiner - bp 1877
Lina Jordan Robertson - bp 1877
Mabel Witter - bp 1877, dis
Samuel O. Willard - bp 1877
Daniel Everett Willard - bp 1877, dis 1891
Evelyn Adell Willard - bp 1877, dis 1891
Mary Lucinda Burdick - bp 1878, d
Mary Emmogene Babcock - bp 1878, d Aug '89
Elbert R. Smith - bp 1878, dis Dec '93
Mrs. Clarrissa Edwards - bp 1878, dis, d Mar 25 '87
Ephraim Allison Curtis - bp 1879, dis Jan 10 '90
Elva Maria Rogers - bp 1879, dis Nov '95
Jasper W. Coller - ad 1879, dis Aug '85
Maria L. Allen - bp 1881, dis Aug 31 '83

Rev. Charles A. Burdick - ad 1882, dis Jan '87
Mrs. Amanda Burdick - ad 1882, dis Jan '87
M. Ardelle Burdick - ad 1882, dis 1887

p. 6

George Clark - bp 1882, excom Sep 2 '83
H. Emmogene Rogers - bp 1882, d
Robert Browning Kenyon - bp 1882, dp Jan 6, 1902
Charles A. Coon - bp 1882, d
Lizzie A. Willard - bp 1882
Arthur L. Johnson - ad 1882, excom Sep '94
Mrs. A. Jane White - ad 1882, d 1897
Mrs. E. Adelle Rogers - ad 1882
Deacon D. B. Stillman - ad 1882, d May 8 '83
Mrs. Sarah A. Stillman - ad 1882, d Jul 30 '86
David C. Green - ad 1882, dis '95, d Feb 11, 1905
Mrs. Alvina Green - ad 1882, dis Mar '95
Deacon Edwin Daniels - ad 1883
Mrs. Abby Jane Daniels - ad 1883, d
Deacon John B. Whitford - ad 1883, d Mar 20, 1901
Mrs. Mary F. Whitford - ad 1883
Lavern Burdick - ad 1883, fell from barn Jun 30, 1914
Addie H. Burdick - ad 1883
Alonzo B. Coon - ad 1884, d Apr '92
Mrs. Eleanor O. Coon - ad 1884, d Dec 7 '86
Mrs. Lavinia M. Coon - ad 1884, d Apr 7 '01
Emmet L. Burdick - ad 1884, dis Feb '96
Ida E. Burdick - ad 1884, dis Feb '96
Bessie Z. Clarke - ad 1884, d May 1, 1900
Georgie F. Sinnette - bp 1884, dis
T. Elvira Kenyon - bp 1884, dp
Lucy Davidson - bp 1884

p. 7

Mrs. Winslow Latham - bp 1885
Loyal Latham - bp 1885, excom Sep '94
Susie T. Babcock - bp 1885, dis Jan, 1902
Arthur Babcock - bp 1885
Cordon Burdick - bp 1885
Lizzie Burdick - bp 1885
Henry Jordan - bp 1885, dis Dec 24 '99
Alford Jordan - bp 1885, ex Dec 24 '99
Robert L. Coon - bp, dis Apr 1901
Markie S. Coon - bp 1885
Daisy Coon - bp 1885
Ivanilla Allen - ad 1886
Floyd B. Wells - bp 1886, dis 1887
Fanny A. Green - bp 1886, dis Aug '92
Emma M. Johnson - bp 1886, d 1898
Magdelia Rogers - bp 1887, d 1932
William H. Stillman - ad 1887, d 1894
Mrs. Susan Stillman - ad 1887, d Jul '89

John B. Gear - ad by testimomy 1887
Rev. L. C. Rogers - ad 1887, dis Nov 3 '88
Mrs. Josephine Rogers - ad 1887, dis Nov 3 '88
Hortense Rogers - ad 1887, dis Nov 3 '88
Mrs. Joanna Brown - ad 1888, d Nov '99
Mrs. Mary C. Cass - ad 1888
Clark W. Green - ad 1888
Nellie Perkins - ad 1888
Mrs. Chloe Perkins - ad 1888, d 1895
Lois T. McKee - bp 1888
Lottie Hamilton - bp, d 1889
Mary Clark - bp 1888

p. 8

Grace A. Burdick - bp 1888, excom 1895
Nina Daniels - bp 1888
William H. Daniels - ad 1888
Katie Daniels - ad 1888
Mary L. Allen - bp 1888
Florence Covey - bp 1888, excom 1894
Percy Clarke - bp 1888
Rev. H. B. Lewis - ad 1885, dis Apr 1 '91
Mrs. H. B. Lewis - ad 1885, dis Apr 1 '91
Harry Enos - bp 1889
Ernest A. Wells - bp 1889
Floyd Burdick - bp 1889
Elwood Green - bp 1889
Elery Burdick - bp 1889, dis Feb 1896
Bessie Burdick - bp 1889, dis Feb '96
J. Fred Whitford - bp 1889
Gordie Green - bp 1889, dp Jan 6, 1902
Louie Clarke - bp 1889
D. C. Willard - bp 1891
Daniel Cass - bp 1891
Grace Wilcox - bp 1892, dis Nov 28 '96
Rachael Wardner - ad ??? 1892
Mary Burdick - bp 1892, dis Nov 1898
George Witter - bp 1892
Luella Cass - bp 1892, dis
Belle Mix - bp 1892, dis May 1903

p. 9

Mrs. Sarah S. Wardner - ad 1892, dis Dec 1901
Thomas B. Wardner - bp 1892
John C. Crandall - ad 1892
Byron Frank Whitford - ad 1892
John Morton Esklemon - bp 1892, ex
Nellie V. Evans - bp 1892
Avis E. Jordan - bp 1892
Elizabeth Tinker - bp 1892
William E. Coon - bp 1892, ex
Ferris Whitford - bp 1892
Lorena White - bp 1892

Clarence Clarke - bp 1892, dis Dec '99
Leonard Coon - ad 1892, d Jun 1904
Sarah Ann Coon - ad 1892, d Jan 1896
Esther A. Dye - ad 1892, d Apr 1895
Lora Coon Stillman - ad 1892
Frank Stillman - ad 1892
Charles Hubble - ad 1892, d
Cornelia Hubble - ad 1892, d 1898
Rev. M. B. Kelly - ad 1892, dis Jan '96
Mrs. M. B. Kelly - ad 1892, dis Jan '96
William Threlkeld - ad 1892, dis
Rachel Summerbell - ad 1894

p. 10

Eugene Perkins - bp 1893
Florence McKee - bp 1893
Frances McKee - bp 1893
Mabel Lasher - bp 1894, excom Aug 12 '94
Addie Lasher - bp 1894, excom Aug 12 '94
Rose Saddler - bp 1894
Walter Allen - bp 1894, excom Mar 26, 1905
Lula Sinnett - bp 1894, dp
Ronald A. Sinnett - bp 1894, excom Mar 12, 1905
Mrs. Laura Jordon - bp
Emma Green - bp 1894
Rena Daniels - bp 1894
Bessie Latham - bp 1894
C. D. McKee - adp 1894, excom Mar 26, 1905
Floyd S. Cartwright - ad 1894, dp Jan 6, 1902
Enoch A. Crandall - ad 1895, restored
 after 40 yrs of wandering
Curtis Skinner - bp 1895
Lena Skinner - bp 1895
Myrta Skinner - bp 1895, excom Mar 26, 1905
Menzo Lanphear - bp 1895, dis Feb '96
Myra Davidson - bp 1895

p. 11

Rev. G. B. Shaw - ad 1895, dis Oct 2 '97
Nellie E. Shaw - ad 1895, dis Oct 24 '97
Eliza B. Fries - ad 1895
Charles M. Mix - ad 1895
Roselia Lovinnia Mix - ad 1895
Rev. W. D. Gardiner - ad 1895, excom
 Mar 26, 1905
Mrs. W. D. Gardiner - ad 1895, excom
 Mar 26, 1905
Mrs. Fannie A. Green Lanphere - ad 1895,
 dis Feb '96
Nathan Wardner - ad 1896
Ethan Rex Willard - bp 1896
Geniveve McKee - bp 1896
Juliett Babcock w/o Dr. B. Babcock - bp 1896

Mrs. A. Janett Fuller - ad 1897
Simeon B. Smith - ad 1897, dis Dec 1901
Gertrude Coats - bp 1897
Bertha Coats - bp 1897
Lelia Davidson - bp 1897
Jessie Irish - bp 1897
Mary Irish - bp 1897

Hurbert Cass - bp 1897
Mrs. Elizabeth L. Daniels - bp 1897
Miss Chloe S. Clarke - bp 1897, dis 1899
Rev. W. D. Burdick - ad 1897, dis 1905 to Farina IL
Mrs. W. D. Burdick - ad 1897, dis 1905

CRR 19x.49.3   vault
Friendship SDRecords 1830-1957
IMS:1995

Richburg SDB Church 1827-
Richburg, Allegany Co. NY
First called Bolivar, then Wirt, Richburg in 1861

Constituent Members

Ephrain Rogers - ex
Elijah Fuller - d Jun 24, 1802
Ransom Gilbert - 1834
Nathan R. Bliven - d 1839
Clark D. Rogers - dis
Calvin Messenger - d Feb 10, 1848
Phiney L. Evans - ex 1833
Abigail Fuller - d Mar 24, 1847

Prudence Gilbert
Lucinda Bliven - gone off
Lucinda Wheelock - ex
Martha Messenger - d Jun 7, 1832
Achsa Messenger - dis
Roxy Messenger
Polly Evans - d May 5, 1843
Cloe Rogers - gone

Members

Harvey C. Foster - ex 1842
Luther Messenger
John Scott - ex
Nathan B. Scott - ex
Elias Scott - ex
Erastus Scott - ex, rest
Daniel Williams - d Jun 25, 1845
Abel Root Jr - ex
Jonas Scott - ex
David Twist
Leander Scott

Catherine Foster
Polly Scott - d Sep 22, 1847
Phelinia Scott
Artimissa Scott - ex
Emily Scott - ex
Louisa Scott - gone out
Mary Williams
Ann Brown - dis
Meranda Fuller - ad 1829, d Aug 8, 1845
Nancy Twist - ad 1830, dis
Hannah Rogers

CRR.15.1 Vault
Richburg NY SDB Church Records 1827-1843
IMS:1995

Richburg Membership List 1837-1868

p.2

Nathan Maxson - ad 1831, dis 1866
Nathan Pierce - ad 1832, dis 1843
Jobe Maxson - ad 1832, dis 1840
Moses Maxson - dis 1840
David Maxson
Joseph Maxson - ad 1832, d Mar 21, 1834
Rowland I. Crandall - ad 1836, dis 1836
James L. Scott - ex
Edwin Fuller - dis 1853
Elias Scott - ex 1851, rest
Erastus Scott - dp, rest
Rowse Babcock - ad Feb 21, 1841, dis
Jared Maxson - ad Feb 26, 1841, d
Ethel Steward - d Spring 1844

Schuyler Saunders - ad Feb 1842
John S. Ayars - gone out
David Campbell - bp Feb 25, 1843, ex
Manville Babcock - bp Feb 25, 1843, ex
C. L. Williams - bp Feb 25, 1843
Sally Pierce - dis 1843
Polly Allen - dis
Nancy Maxson - d Jan 16, 1865
Elenor Maxson - d 1852
Isabel R. Maxson - dis 1853
Susan Crandall - ad 1836, dis
Sylvia Maxson - ad 1837
Martha Maxson - ad 1837, d
Cinderilla Scott
Polly Maxson - dis 1855

Permelia Rogers Ballard
Ann Eliza Randolph - gone
Judah Coon - dis
Emily Coon - dis
Zilpha Messinger
Harriet Griffith Evans - ad 1842
Amy Maxson - dis
Lucinda Babcock - dis
Lucy Potter - dis 1866
Sally Messenger - bp, gone
Abby Jane Daniels

p. 3
John B. Cottrell - ad 1844
James Maxson - ad 1845, d Sep 7, 1866
James S. Maxson - bp 1845, gone
Zurial Campbell - ad 1845, dis
Augustus Kenyon - ad 1845, d Jan 20, 1854
Thomas E. Babcock - ad 1846, dis
Gilbert E. Gillett - bp 1847, d Oct 9, 1853
John Scott - rest, d Mar 22, 1853
Clark T. Champlin
George W. Meriatt - ad 1850, dis 1855
John P. Dye - ad 1850
Edwin Daniels - ad 1850
Ransom Fuller - rest 1850
Alanson Rogers - bp 1850
Morris H. Coats - bp 1850
George W. Trapp - ad 1857
Isac Day - bp 1852
George B. Case - bp 1852
George L. Maase - gone
Ambrose J. Truman - dis 1852
Sally Gilbert Willcox
Betsey Ann Willcox - ex
Harriet N. Willcox - ex
Nancy H. Wiicox - ex
Lucinia Gilbert - bp, dis
Hannah Kenyon - bp
Eunace Cottrell - ad 1844, dis
Amy Campbell - ad 1845, dis
Hannah Scott Babcock - ad 1846
Mary Cottrell - bp 1847, dis
Nancy Day - bp 1847, ex
Huldah L. Truman - dis
Laura A. Champlain
Mary J. Kenyon - bp 1850
Asenath W. Scott - bp 1850, dp
Susan A. Dye - ad 1850
Achso Randolph - ad 1850
Rosina T. Fuller - ad 1850
Phebe Evans - bp 1850, dis
Francis A. Cottrell - ad 1852
Melissa M. Maxson - dp

p. 4
Ephraim R. Reed - dp
George Hamilton - dp
William H. Stillman - ad 1854, dis 1868
Joseph Case - ad 1855
William M. Truman - ad 1855, dis
Ethel Rogers - ad 1855
Almond Rogers Jr - ad 1855, gone
Oscar Kenyon - bp 1857, gone
Augustus Ryno - bp 1857, excom 1858
Amos Satterlee - dis 1852
Rev. Leman Andrus - ad 1853, dis 1862
Jacob Crandall - ad 1853, dis 1866
Dea. Nathan Truman - dis 1853

p. 5
Susan A. Maxson - bp 1852, dis 1866
Sarah A. Trapp - bp 1852, dp, dis
Sarah Morris Kenyon - bp 1852, dis 1865
Phebe A. Rightingbark - bp 1852, dis 1865
Harriet Green - bp 1852, gone off
Emma L. S. E. Cottrell - bp 1852, dis
Augusta Cottrell
Sarah Smith - dp
Catherine Rogers
Betsey Lebar - dp
Elizabeth Satterley - ad 1852, d May 5, 1853
Eliza Hamilton - ad 1852, d Apr 26, 1854
Martha Green - ad 1853, gone off
Susan Stillman - ad 1856, dis 1858
Mary Case - ad 1855
Elozia Truman Moose - ad 1855, dp
G. Lavern Maxson Cleaveland - ad 1855
    d Nov 11, 1863
Mary Lewis - ad 1855, dp
Martha Messinger McGibeny - ad 1855
Amanda Randolph - ad 1855
Juliett Rogers Rhyno - ad 1855

p. 6
P. C. Cartwright - bp Sep 1857
Ira Lanphere - ad 1857
I. B. McGibeny - ad 1858, dis 1858
A. Randolph Ryno - ad 1858 excom 1868
Gerome Reed - ad 1858, ex 1858, rest 1859

p. 7
Sally O. Maxson Phillips
Harriet Maxson - dis 1866
Sarah M. Reed - bp 1857, d Nov 58
Garphelia Maxson - bp 1857
Joanna Ryno - bp 1857
Elizabeth Coats - bp 1857

Lidia Maxson - bp 1857, dis 1866
Martha A. Lanphere Kenyon - ad 1857
Welthy Ann Andrus - ad 1858, dis 1863
Cordelia Williams - bp 1858
Mary Ann Tailor - ad 1858
Lieten Tailor - ad 1858
Sarah Eddy - bp, dp, d Feb 3, 1864
Laura Gellitt - bp, d Feb 3, 1864

p. 8
Elder J. P. Hunting - ad 1858, dis
Runyon Randolph - ad 1859
Clark Kenyon - ad 1862
Orlando Burdick - bp 1863
Byron Maxson - bp 1863
Casius M. Maxson - bp 1863, killed in battle before Petersburg, Jun 14, 1864
I. L. Cottrell
M. Rose Cottrell, G. M.
Frederick W. Evans - dis 1865
John D. Woodward - dp
A. B. Cottrell - bp 1863
William L. Burdick - ad 1864
Rhoda Burdick - ad 1864

p. 9
Senett S. Hunting - ad 1868, d
Mrs. Ruth Reed - ad 1858
Frances Fuller - ad May 1861
Schyler Maxson - ad 1862, d Mar 1863
Lohaney Burdick - bp 1863
Mary Messinger - bp 1863
Edwin Gilbert - ad 1864, dis 1866
Oscar Kenyon - ad 1864, dis 1866
Hellen Kenyon - ad 1864
Lucy B. Jacobs - ad 1864, dp
Dea. D. B. Stillman - 1865

p. 10
Elder Leman Andrus - ad 1866, dis 1868
Welthy Ann Andrus - ad 1866, dis 1866
Orsemus G. Stillman - ad 1866
Mary J. Stillman - ad 1866
Edwin L. Bliss - ad 1866
Sarah Bliss - ad 1866
Charles Saunders - ad 1866
Mrs. Finetta Saunders - ad 1866
Angelica Dye - 1866
Angelia Kenyon - ad 1866, d
Edelia Babcock - ad 1866
Eunice Cottrell - ad 1866
Edwin Gilbert - ad Feb 10, 186
Harriet Gilbert - ad 1867

p. 11
S. C. Stillman - ad 1867
Theresa C. Stillman - 1867
Philander B. Case - bp 1868
Charles R. Saunders - ad 1868
James O. Irish - 1868
Nelson O. Stillman - 1868
Mary L. Cartwright - ad 1868
M. Eva Burdick - ad 1868
Lovina E. Champlin - ad 1868
Mary R. Griffin - 1868

p. 12
Alice E. Williams - bp 1868
L. Adelbert Champlin - bp 1868
Albert M. Maxson - bp 1868
E. S. Fuller - bp 1868
Mrs. A. Jenett Fuller - bp 1868
Charlie F. Fuller - ad 1868
W. W. Coats - bp 1868
A. Ray Coats - ad 1868
Mrs. A. R. Coats - ad 1868
Rev. G. J. Crandall - ad 1868
Elizabeth Crandall - ad 1868
Samuel Stebbins

CRR 1991.15.22 Vault
Richburg SDB Church Records 1837-1868
IMS:1995

Richburg Membership List 1868

p. 17
Samuel D. Rogers - d Sep 18, 1879
Catherine Foster
Luther Messenger
Mary Scott
Hannah Rogers - d Feb 1, 1988
Moses Maxson - d nov 14, 1850
Martha Maxson
David Maxson - d Apr 27, 1877
Jane Maxson
C. S. Williams
Permillia Ballard
Zilpha Messenger
Harriet Griffin
Abby Jane Daniels - d
John B. Cottrell - d Jan 27, 1873
Eunice Cottrell
John P. Dye
Edwin Daniels
Ransom Fuller - Sep 16, 1872
Alanson Rogers
Morris Coats
Sally Willcox
Hannah M. Kenyon Satterlee
Mary J. Kenyon Palmer
Achsa Randolph

p. 18
Susan A. Dye
Rosina F. Fuller
Francis Cottrell Morrison
Joseph Case - d 1881
Mary Case - d
Ethel P. Rogers
Augusta Cottrell Carter
Catherine Rogers
Martha McGibeny
Amanda Randolph
Juliette Ryno - d 1886
P. C. Cartwright - d May 1918
Sally Phillips, dp
G. A. Smith
Joanna Shaw - dis
Elizabeth Stillman - d 1879
Martha A. Kenyon - dis
C. M. Kenyon - ex 1871
Cordelia Williams

John Runyon Randolph - d
Bryon D. Maxson
H. S. Cottrell - dis 1872
A. B. Cottrell
Ruth Reed
Francis Fuller - d
Mary Skinner
Helen M. Kenyon
Dea. D. B. Stillman - d
Jane Maxson

p. 19
O. G. Stillman - dis
Mary J. Stillman - dis
E. S. Bliss
Sarah M. Bliss
Charles Saunders - d Jan 14, 1876
Finnette Saunders
Angelica Dye Cottrell
Erzelia Babcock - ex
Flora Cottrell Mosher - ad 1877, dis
E. D. Gilbert
H. D. Gilbert
S. C. Stillman
T. C. Stillman
Charles R. Saunders - ex
James O. Irish - 1870

p. 20
T. B. Case - bp 1868
Nelson Stillman - dis
Eva Burdick Pitts - dp
Mary L. Cartwright
Lovina E. Champlin
Mary R. King
Alice Williams Coats
S. A. Champlin - dp
P. B. Case
Albert M. Maxson
E. S. Fuller
Mrs. A. J. Fuller
Charles F. Fuller
W. W. Coats
A. R. Coats
Susan Coats
G. J. Crandall - dis
Elizabeth Crandall - dis
Jane Yarrington - ex Nov 28, 1874

p. 21
Marshall Willcox - ad 1869, dp
Addie A. Willcox - ad 1869, dp
Jerome Reed - ad 1869, d Oct 14, 1875
John Ryno - ad 1869
Mrs. S. A. Stillman - ad 1869
Mrs. Adaline Coats - ad 1870
Amos M. Coats - ad 1870
Willis H. Maxson - ad 1870
Viola M. Coats - ad 1870
Alanson Kenyon - ad 1870
Polly Kenyon - ad 1870
Mrs. Samuel S. Stebbins - ad 1870
Syman A. Stillman - bp 1870, ex
Clarie Reed - bp 1870, dp
Jennie Harrison Gilbert - bp 1870, d 1876
p. 22
William H. Daniels - bp 1871
Willie Saunders - bp 1871
George Stillman - bp 1871
Nathaniel Putman - ad 1871, d
Mary Putman Collins - ad 1871
Cornelia Glover - adp 1871, d Dec 16, 1871
Joseph Messenger - bp 1971
Mrs. Joseph Messinger
Hapreet L. Hoford - ad 1871
Caleb Williams - bp 1871, d Dec 26, 1876
Mrs. A. A. Lewis - bp 1871, d Dec 26, 1876
Francis D. Allen - bp 1874
Mrs. A. M. Coats - bp 1874
Are E. Hood - bp 1874
Ida N. Smith - bp 1874
Ida B. Fuller Hull - bp 1874, dis 1880
Gusta M. Smith White - bp 1874, dis 1880
Ida L. Lanphere - bp 1874, ex 1880
H. P. Hopkins - bp 1874, dis 1881
Oliver Rogers - bp 1874
Fred L. Coats - bp 1874
Randolph Ryno - rest
p. 23
D. C. Green - bp 1874
Lovinia Green - bp 1874
Ida Green Burdick - bp 1874, dis 1876
Mary Ann Ryno - bp 1874
Maria Davis - ad 1875, dis 1881
M. D. Crandall - ad 1875
Sarah T. Crandall - bp 1875
Mrs. Eliza Mix - bp 1876, d
Mrs. Belle Cottrell - bp 1876

Katie Daniels - bp 1876
E. Adele White Rogers - bp 1876
W. F. White - bp 1876
Myrtie S. Bliss - 1876
Marion Allen - bp 1876
Prudence Saunders Smith - bp 1876
Finnette Saunders - bp 1876
Clarence F. Smith - bp 1876
Hettie V. Burdick - bp 1876
p. 24
Ralph G. Wells - bp 1876, dp
Thomas S. George - bp 1876, ex 1879
Edwin E. Coats - bp 1876
Willie M. Coats - bp 1876
Mary E. Coats - bp 1876
Ida Stillman Burdick - bp 1876
Simeon B. Smith - ad 1876
Minerva E. Smith - ad 1876
Eva M. Green - ad 1876
Mrs. Jane Allen - ad 1876
John T. King - ad 1876
Hattie Green - ad 1876
Charles Crandall - ad 1876
Mrs. Sophia Burdick - ad 1876
Mr. L. C. Burdick - ad 1876
Eld. James Summerbell - ad 1876
Rachel Summerbell - ad 1876
p. 25
Mr. Cyrus Cartwight - bp 1876
Mrs. Elvira Cartwright - bp 1876
Miss Matie Rogers - bp 1876
Mr. Samuel Allen - ad 1876, d Jul 18, 1880
Mrs. Roxy Allen - ad 1876
Miss Lozetia Allen - bp 1876
Mrs. Anna E. Saunders - bp 1878
Mrs. Mary Stebbins - bp 1878
Miss Nellie B. Perkins
Mrs. Vina Maxson
Carrie E. Crandall - ad 1877
Harvey Foster - ad 1877, rest
Mr. Andrew Allen - ad 1877
Mrs. Lydia Allen - ad 1877
Mrs. Ida M. Sharks Champlin - bp 1878
p. 26
Hannah Lucetta Cartwright - bp 1877
George Rolla Crandall - bp 1877
Frank M. Crandall - bp 1877
Lovica T. Baker - bp 1877

Edna A. Bliss - bp 1877
Erwin A. Hood - bp 1877
Wesley A. Ryno - bp 1877
Franklin Randolph - bp 1877
Charles Ballard - ad 1878
Mrs. Louisa Davidson - ad 1878
Ida E. Merritt - ad 1878
Mr. Benjamin Vincent - ad 1878
Lewis S. Munroe - ad 1878
Mrs. L. I. Munroe - ad 1878
Mrs. Ida J. Williams - bp 1878
Alice A. Jordan - ad 1878

p. 27
Edwin Miller - ad 1878
Eva I. Miller - ad 1878
Mrs. Mary Randolph - bp 1878
John Hood - 86 yrs old, bp 1879,
    fr Methodist Church, d Sep 4, 1879
Charles L. Harvey Rogers - bp 1879
A. R. Ripley Covey - bp 1879
Warren W. Covey - bp 1879
John N. Covey - bp 1879
p. 28
Mrs. Warren W. Covey - ad 1880

Church Roll Corrected 1890

p. 29
Catherine Foster - d Feb 15, 1884
Luther Messenger - d Mar 30, 1889
Hannah Rogers - d Feb 5, 1888
Martha Maxson - d Oct 12, 1882
Jane Maxson - Jun 6, 1886
C. L. Williams
Permelia Ballard
Harriet Griffin
Abby Jane Daniels - dis 1883
Eunice Cottrell
J. P. Dye - dp 1889
Susan A. Dye - dp 1889
p. 30
Edwin Daniels - dis 1883
Alanson Rogers
Morris H. Coats
Sally Willcox
Hannah M. Satterlee
Mary Satterlee - d Sep 28, 1888
Achsa Randolph - d Dec 11, 1886
Rosina F. Fuller - dis 1882
Francis A. Marvin
Joseph Case - d Jun 13, 1881
Mary Case - d Jan 25, 1884
Ethel P. Rogers
Augusta Carter
p. 31
Catherine Rogers
Amanda Randolph - d
Martha McGibeny
Juliette Rogers Ryno - d Aug 4, 1889
Gaphelia A. Smith Woodward
Cordelia Williams
John R. Randolph - d 1894

Dea. Byron D. Maxson - Fresno CA
A. B. Cottrell - dis
Ruth Reed - d May 10, 1891
Frances Fuller - dis Dec 16, 1882
Mary Skinner
Hellen M. Kenyon - dis 1883
p. 32
D. B. Stillman - dis 1882
E. S. Bliss - dis 1887
Sarah M. Bliss - dis 1887
Mrs. Fenetta Saunders Metz - dis 1886
E. D. Gilbert
H. L. Gilbert - dis 1885
P. B. Case - d
Mary L. Cartwright - dis 1883
Lovina E. Champlin
Mary R. King
Alice Coats
Albert Maxson - dis 1885
E. S. Fuller - d
p. 33
Mrs. A. J. Fuller
Charles F. Fuller - dp 1890
W. W. Coats
A. R. Coats - d Jun 8, 1888
Mrs. Susan Coats
Mrs. Adela A. Willcox Remington; Hornellsville
John Ryno - d
Mrs. S. A. Stillman - dis 1882
Mrs. Adaline Coats
Amos Coats
Willis A. Maxson - dis 1885
Viola M. Trask - dis 1887
Polly Kenyon - d Jul 9, 1895

p. 34
Samuel L. Stebbins - dp 1890
Charles Satterlee - d Mar 29, 1892
W. H. Daniels - dis Jun 2, 1888
Willie A. Saunders
George W. Saunders
Mary L. Allen - dis 1892
Joseph Messenger
Ed Emerson
Elizabeth Messenger - d Jul 19, 1889
Harriet L. Head
Caleb Willcox - d
Francis D. Allen - dis Dec 16, 1882
Anna M. Coats
Ary E. Hood

p. 35
Mrs. Ida M. Hood
Mrs. Gusta M. White - d Jul 24, 1891
Horace F. Hopkins - dis Apr 22, 1881
Olivar Rogers - dp 1895
Fred L. Coats
Randolph Ryno - d Dec 30, 1887; Alfred
David C. Green - dis 1882
Lovina Green - dis 1882
Mary Ann Ryno - d
Maria Davis - dis 1881
Morton D. Crandall
Sarah T. Crandall - d
Mrs. Bell Cottrell - dis

p. 36
Mrs. Katie Daniels - dis 1888
Mrs. E. Adell Rogers - dis 1882
W. F. White
Marion Allen - excom 1888
Prudence Smith - dis 1885
Mirta S. Bliss - dis 1881
Finetta Saunders Skinner - dis 1886
Clarence F. Smith - d Sep 22, 1888
Hettie V. Burdick - dis 1884
Edwin D. Coats - dis 1884
Willie M. Coats
Mary E. Coats
Ida Stillman Burdick - excom 1881

p. 37
Simeon B. Smith - dis 1885
Minerva E. Smith - dis 1885
Eva M. Green - excom 1885
Jane Allen - excom 1888
John T. King
Hattie Green - excom 1885
Charles Crandall
Lewis C. Burdick - excom 1885, rest
Sophia Burdick - Olean
Rev. James Summerbell - dis 1882
Rachel Summerbell - dis 1882
Cyrus Cartwright
Elvira Cartwright

p. 38
Matie A. Rogers Moses
Roxy Allen Sherman
Lydia Allen Maxson - dis 1885
Carrie E. Crandall - dis
Harvey C. Foster - age 83, d Sep 19, 1886
Andrew J. Allen - d
Lydia Allen Maxson
M. Woodward - Florida
Sue Martin Woodward
Ida M. Champlin - excom
Anna E. Saunders
Mary Stebbins - Bolivar
Vina Maxson - California
Nellie P. Perkins - dis 1888
H. Linceta Cartwright - Bolivar

p. 39
George Rollo Crandall
Frank M. Crandall - d
Lovica T. Baker Harvey - dis 1884
Edna A. Bliss - dis 1887
Irwin A. Hood - dp 1890
Wesley A. Ryno
Franklin Randolph
Charles Ballard - d
Louisa Davidson - dis 1888
Ida E. Merrett - Olean
Benjamin M. Vincent
Lewis S. Munroe - d
Mrs. I. I. Munroe - gone

p. 40
Ida J. Willcox
Alice A. Jordan - d May 9, 1882
Edwin Miller - excom 1888
Eva L. Miller - excom 1888
John S. Brosheion - excom 1881
Mrs. Mary Randolph
Charles L. Harvey - dis 1888

A. R. Ripley Covey
Warren W. Covey - d
John N. Covey
Laura D. Covey w/o W.W.
John B. Whitford - ad 1881, dis 1883
Mary E. Whitford - ad 1881, dis 1883

p. 41
William A. Rose - ad 1883, dis
Delilah Rose - ad 1883, dis
Charles Stillman - ad 1883, dis 1884
Jennie A. Stillman - ad 1883, dis 1884
Rev. J. E. Backus - ad 1883, dis 1885
Mrs. Lucy A. Backus - ad 1883, dis 1885
Lincoln G. Backus - ad 1883, dis 1885
J. E. Harvey Backus - ad 1883, dis 1883
Mrs. Cornelia Bullock - ad 1883, dis
Ida E. Palmiter Millard Brafford - ad 1884
Mary E. Palmiter Burdick - ad 1884, dis 1894
Mrs. Mary L. Griffin - ad 1884

p. 42
Mrs. J. A. Lyons - bp Mar 28, 1884; Silver Creek MI
Miss Belle Witter - bp 1884
Mr. E. L. Maxson - ad Sep 6, 1884
Rev. Byron E. Fisk - ad 1885, dis 1886
Mrs. Alice Fisk - ad 1885
Edith Cartwright - bp 1885, dp 1890
Mr. John T. Rogers - ad 1884
Mrs. Linda R. Rogers - 1884
Rosina T. Fuller - ad 1885, d Dec 25, 1890
Francis Fuller - d Oct 30, 1885

p. 43
Mrs. Flora Cartwright - ad 1886
Mary Delong - bp 1886
Emma Cartwright - bp 1886
William R. Maxson - ad 1887

Estelle G. Keller - ad 1889
Welthy A. Riddle - ad 1889
An Satterlee - ad 1889, d Jan 1892
Susanna Lanphere - ad 1889
Abby A. Maxson - ad 1887
Emma Maxson - ad 1887
Byron E. Maxson - ad 1889
Libbie Maxson - ad 1889
Marian L. Keller - ad 1889

p. 44
Samuel Crandall - ad 1889
Alzina Crandall - ad 1889, d May 30, 1894
Mrs. A. E. Palmer - ad 1889; Alfred
W. L. Bardeen - bp 1889
Ella N. Bardeen - ad 1889
Charles M. Mix - bp 1889
Rosalia R. Mix - bp 1893
Dea. T. B. Bardeen - ad 1889, dis
Mrs. S. L. Bardeen - ad 1889, dis

p. 45
Mabell King - bp 1892, d
Bernice Cottrell - bp 1892
Annie Sullivan - bp 1892, dis
Mrs. Mary Hood - bp 1892
Walter Brown - bp 1892
Benjamin Hood - bp 1893
Charles Saunders - bp 1893
Rev. M. G. Stillman - ad 1893
Marcella Stillman - ad 1893
Lelia C. Stillman - ad 1893
Harold C. Stillman - ad 1893
Lennie Bassett - ad 1893
Prudence Smith - ad 1893
Weltha Saunders - ad 1893
O. Griffin - ad 1896

(ed note: These books were in bad condition; S's and L's were particularly hard to decipher.)

CRR 1991.15.7 Vault
Richburg Membership Lists 1868-1941
IMS:1995

III. THE GENESEES

First Genesee SDB Church 1827-
Little Genesee, Allegany Co. NY
First called Cuba, then Genesee in 1832, then First Genesee in 1835

Constituent Members

p. 5

Joseph Maxson - d Jan 28, 1856
Benjamin Maxson - rj
Ezekiel Crandall - d Jul 15, 1855
Henry P. Green - dis 1848
Joel Maxson - d Feb 28, 1865
Amos Green - ad 1827, d Mar 25, 1885
Esther Green - d Dec 1862
Lydia Maxson - d Jun 15, 1843
Susan Crandall - d Apr 29, 1861
Joseph Wells - d
Lydia Wells - d Mar 26, 1861
Lucy Green - d May 9, 1846
Phebe Maxson - dis
Nancy Kenyon - d

Members

George G. Kenyon - rj
Sally Kenyon - rj 1844
Lucy C. Maxson - dis
Jabez Burdick - rj, rest 1854, 79 yrs
Sally Burdick - d May 1846
Henry C. Crandall - ad 1827, d Jun 9, 1892
Joseph Wells Jr - d Sep 1855
George Potter - called to diaconate 1828 dis 1854
Betsy Potter - dis 1854

1830 -- 1835
Joel Crandall - ad 1832
David Maxson - ad 1832, rj Oct 26, 1849
Penelope Maxson - ad 1832, d
Mary Maxson - ad 1832
Sally Maxson - d Sep 28, 1855
Enoch K. Maxson - dis
Peleg Babcock - ad 1830, absent
Paul Ennis - ad 1830, d May 29, 1855
Ebenezer D. Bliss

p. 6
Edwin Stillman - rj
Clarke S. Wells - dis 1870
Martha Bliss - d Nov 1861
Mary Tew - bp, rj
Mary Potter - bp, d 1840
Emma Potter - bp, d Sep 6, 1852
Jason L. Wells - bp, absent
Jared Maxson - bp, rj 1857
Polly Burdick - bp, d Aug 11, 1861
Lucy E. Green - d 1831
Catherine Boss - bp, rj
Elliot Smith

Betsey Smith - dis
Mercy Maxson - d Jan 23, 1863
John Tanner - d Sep 5, 1870
Clarissa Tanner - d Dec 15, 1873
Ethan P. Crandall - dis
Electa Crandall - dis
Lucinda Babcock - d
Joseph S. Crandall - dis
Oliva Crandall - dis
Asa Langworthy - d Aug 22, 1856
Thomas Tew - licensed to preach
Mariah E. Stillman - rj
George Potter Jr - d Mar 25, 1856
Lucy Maryott - rj 1844
Willet Maxson - d Oct 28, 1854
Jabez Burdick - rj
Palermo Lackey - dis
Mary Ann Kenyon Randolph
Daniel B. Wells Jr - rj
Samuel Wells - d
Huldah Crandall
Ann B. Langworthy - absent, rj 1857
Asa A. Langworthy - d May 4, 1844
Phineas Stillman - dis 1851
Jeremiah F. Burdick - rj, rest
Lucinda Ennis Crandall

p. 7
Thomas Maxson - d Sep 5, 1852
Joseph Boss
Mathew Green - rj Sep 1840
Alonzo B. Coon
Orenzo Coon - dis

Henry Smith - dis
Clarke G. Stillman - rj, d Dec 1852
Electra Stillman - dis 1852
Sylvia Palmer - dis
Harriet Edwards - d Feb 21, 1894
William P. Langworthy
Abel G. Burdick
Nancy Burdick
Laura Maxson
Susan Crandall 2nd - dis
Dennis Saunders - dis
Margaret Saunders - d
Ruth G. Langworthy - d May 1863
Zacheus B. Maxson - d Nov 1868
Temperance Maxson - d Sep 11, 1858
Eliza Crandall - dis 1858
Mary Maxson How
Warren Hyde - bp
Ann Hyde - bp
Walter H. Lackey - rj
Joseph L. Stillman
Andrew Barber - dis
Nancy Barber - dis
Susan Smith - dis
Cynthia E. Crandall - dis
George Crandall - dis
Julia Crandall
Jairus Crandall
Mathew B. Maxson - d 1845
Daniel Smith - dis
Charles Smith - dis
Harvy Smith - dis
Charles Satterlee - dis
George Merit Jr - dis

p. 8

Malissa Coon - d Nov 1860
Benjamin Maryott - rj Dec 26, 1856
Charles Maryott - absent, rj Apr 1845
Eliza Bliss
George Maryott - rj 1844
Lucy Maryott - rj 1844
Nancy Coon - d
Almeron D. Stillman - dis
Hannah Stillman - dis
Albert B. Crandall - dis
Hampton C. Crandall - dis
William A. Crandall - dis
Sally M. Crandall - dis
Rowland Coon - dis
Sally Coon - dis
Elizabeth Satterlee - dis
Oliver Champlin - dis
Clarke Saunders - absent, d
Betsey Saunders - dis, d
Roena Drake - absent
Rosina Satterlee - dis
Eleanor Sheldon - dis
Sarah Ann Champlain - dis
Fanny Crandall - dis
Elias J. Maxson - dis
Rachel Maxson - dis
Archibald Smith - dis
Hazard H. Sheldon - rj
Fanny Eaton - dis
Stedman Eaton - dis
Harriet Nye - absent, dis
Betsey Nye - d Mar 18, 1855
Ann Nye - bp, absent, d
Francis Ennis - bp
Sally Green - bp, d Dec 15, 1849
Clark Rogers - absent, dis
Lydia Rogers - d Apr 1845
Varnum Maxson - absent, dis
Laura Ann Maxson - absent, dis
Sally Maxson - ad 1836, absent, dis

p. 9

Daniel M. Crandall - ad 1837, absent, dis 1849
Lewis Coon - bp 1838
Emily Coon - bp 1838
George Buten - bp 1838, dis
Edwin Langworthy - bp 1838, d May 31, 1850
Mary Maxson 2nd - bp 1838, dis
Eliza Crandall - ad 1838, d Apr 1847
Fanny Babcock - bp 1838, dis
Eliza Maxson - bp 1838
Nancy Maxson - dis 1869
Lydia Wells 2nd - bp 1838
John Edwards - ad 1838
Martha Crandall - ad 1838, absent, d Jul 28, 1858
Sarah Crandall - ad 1838, d Apr 1845
Daniel M. Burdick - bp 1838, absent, dis 1855
Amos Maryott - bp 1838, rj
David Bliss - bp 1838
Elizabeth Potter - bp 1838, dis 1852
Oliver Langworthy - bp 1838, absent
Abigail Langworthy - bp 1838, dis
Sarah F. Clawson - bp 1838
George Tanner - bp 1838, dis 1866
Thomas H. Green - bp 1838

Daniel Edwards - ad 1845
Louis Edwards - ad 1838, d Mar 24, 1852
Nancy C. Burdick - ad 1838
Francis G. Green - ad 1838, dis Dec 15, 1851
Avis Hall - ad 1839, dis 1851
John A. Langworthy - ad 1839
Eliza Langworthy - ad 1839, d Jun 24, 1860
Emma S. Langworthy - ad 1839, absent, dis '61
E. Rogers Crandall - ad 1839
Paul M. Vincent - bp 1840, dis
Samuel P. Crandall - bp 1840, absent, dis 1887
Eden Burdick - bp 1840
Zacheus P. Green - bp 1840, dis
Abram Stanard - bp 1840, dis
Alton Maxson - bp 1840, absent, rj 1844

p. 10

Stillman Hall - bp 1840, d Apr 1847
Edward Burdick - bp 1840, dis
James Maxson - bp 1840, d Sep 3, 1854
Benjamin Kenyon - bp 1840, absent, rj 1857
Rebecca Stillman - bp 1840, d Dec 1, 1865
Mary Burdick - bp 1840
Mary Ann Maxson - bp 1840
Sardinia Hall - bp 1840, d 1843
Sarah E. Langworthy - bp 1840, rj 1868
Esther Wells - ad 1840, dis 1870
Azuba Davy - ad 1841, dis
Joseph Stillman - ad 1841, d Apr 11, 1855
Ruth Kenyon - ad 1841
Susan R. Langworthy - ad 1841, dis 1869
Marilla Stanard - ad 1841, d May 1847
Wealthy Hall - ad 1841
Hannah Stillman - ad 1841, d
Ezra Buten - bp 1841, dis
Ira J. Burdick - bp 1841
Welcome Maryott - bp 1841, rj 1852
William Hornblower - bp 1841, absent, dis 1852
Harriet Langworthy - bp 1841, dis
Emma Wells - bp 1841
Eliza Saunders - bp 1841, dis
Sarah T. Bliss - bp 1841
Andrew Norris - bp 1841, rj 1846
Perry Hall - bp 1841, d 1845
Lyman Saunders - bp 1841, absent, d
Abby E. Stillman - bp 1841, absent, rj 1856
Elizabeth Burdick - widow, ad 1840,
   d Feb 27, 1856
Abigail Burdick - ad 1840, dis
Electa Coon - bp 1840

Elizabeth Burdick - ad 1840, d
Avory Coon - ad 1840
John Maxson - ad 1840, absent
Calista Maxson - ad 1840
Esther Hall - ad 1840, d Jun 19, 1875
Lovina Stillman - ad 1840

p. 11

Eliza Langworthy - bp 1840, dis 1871
Julia Ann Maxson - bp 1840
Fanny Potter - ad 1841
Mary Ann Buten - ad 1841, absent, d Oct 18, 1844
William Sweet - ad 1841, absent, d
Hannah Saunders - ad 1841, dis
Martha Barber - ad 1842, absent, d
Harriet E. Maxson - ad 1842
Elizabeth Babcock - ad 1843, rj Feb 21, 1851
Eunice Lackey - ad 1843
James B. Langworthy - ad 1843, absent, dis
Briant Cartwright - ad 1843, dis 1871
Elhonah Babcock - ad 1843, absent, dis 1850
James Root - ad 1843, rj 1846
William L. Bowler - bp 1843
Joel B. Crandall - bp 1843
Albert Crandall - bp 1843
Daniel A. Langworthy - bp 1843, rj 1866
John Stewart - bp 1843, absent, rj
Henry Rogers - bp 1843, bp 1843,
   d Andersonville prison 1864
William W. Crandall - bp 1843, dis Sep 29, 1871
Albert Campbell - bp 1843, abent, rj 1852
James Champlain - bp 1843, d
Olivar Champlain - ad 1843, d
Polly Champlain - ad 1843, d 1857 or 1858
Wait S. Burdick - ad 1844
Sarah Ann Green - bp 1844, dis 1851
Susan Tanner - bp 1844, dis 1857
Lucy Crandall - bp 1844
Loira Maryott - ad 1844, d Apr 29, 1855
Abby Edwards - bp 1844, dis 1860
Frances Rogers - bp 1844, d Oct 31, 1852
Eld. S. S. Griswold - ad 1844, dis
Almy Griswold - ad 1844, dis

p. 12

Charles Ward - ad 1844, rj 1850
Daniel Potter - ad 1844
Rebecca Potter - ad 1844
Daniel Crandall - ad 1844, dis
Benjamin F. Burdick - bp 1844
Emeline Burdick - bp 1844, d Sep 1863

Julia Ann Crandall - bp 1844
Semantha Maxson - ad 1845, d 1867
Betsey Burdick - ad 1847, dis 1880
Eleanor Coon - bp 1848
Eld. James Bailey - ad 1848, dis 1854
Tacy Bailey w/o James - ad 1848, dis 1854
Lucy Wells - ad 1848, d Dec 21, 1864
Leander W. Lewis - ad 1864
Clarissa L. Lewis w/o Leander - ad 1884
Angeline Barber - ad 1849
Polly Coon - ad 1849
Eliza Ann Coon - bp 1849
Eliza Boss - bp 1849, d Feb 6, 1857
Betsey Lackey - bp 1849, dis 1866
Martin Babcock - bp 1849, dis, rest
Abigail Burdick - bp 1849, dis 1858
Abby Bliss - bp 1849
Cornelia Coon - bp 1849
Mary A. Maxson - bp 1849, rj 1859
Sarah Ann Rogers - ad 1849, dis 1869
Deidama Burdick - ad 1850, d Jun 30, 1886
Mary Jane Green - bp 1850, d Oct 26, 1852
Charles J. Bliss - bp 1851, d 1863
William Henry Crandall - bp 1851,
 d in battle 1864
Isaac C. Tanner - bp 1851, d Nov 1862
George H. Crandall - bp 1851
Edwin S. Bliss - bp 1851, dis 1965
Luther Green - bp Mar 1862
Albert Tanner - bp 1851, d Feb 28, 1859
William B. Bliss - bp 1851, d Jan 28, 1862
James B. Maryott - bp 1851, d rj 1855
Eliza Ann Barber - bp 1851

p. 13
Harriet Tanner - ad 1851
Marion Crandall - ad 1851, dis 1870
William H. Stillman - bp 1852, dis 1854
Hiram Cornwell - ad 1853, dis 1854
Hannah Cornwell - ad 1853, d Apr 24, 1856
Fanny Cornwell - ad 1853, d Jan 5, 1868
George Lewis - ad 1853, dis 1863
Susannah Lewis - ad 1853, dis 1863
E. Euphemia Crandall - ad 1853, dis 1871
Laura Tanner - bp 1854, dis 1869
Marion Stannard - bp 1854
Laura A. Green - bp 1854
Wealthy A. Burdick - bp 1854
Eld. Thomas B. Brown - ad 1854
Margaret A. Brown - ad 1854
Almira Pringle - bp 1854

Albert R. Crandall - bp 1854, dis 1866
John Crandall - bp 1854
Martin W. Babcock - ad 1854
Mary K. Babcock - ad 1854
Daniel M. Burdick - ad 1854
Sally Burdick - ad 1854
Ralph C. Langworthy - ad 1855, dis 1857
Henry P. Saunders - ad 1855, dis 1857
Mary A. Saunders - ad 1855, dis 1857
Salina N. Coon - bp 1855, rj 1866
Clarissa Edwards - bp 1855, rj 1866
Arminda Lewis - bp 1857, rj Jan 24, 1862
Jane C. Wells - bp 1857, rj 1858
Mary Brown - bp 1857, rj 1862
Daniel L. Corbon - bp 1857
Sophronia Lackey - bp 1857, dis 1865
Adelia M. Maxson - bp 1857, dis 1870
Caroline M. Hall - bp 1857, dis 1870
Huldah A. Stetson - bp 1857
Abby Augusta Wells - bp 1857
Sophronia Lewis - bp 1857, d Feb 17, 1864

p. 14
Martha Ann Lanphere - bp 1857
Susan Mariah Boss - bp 1857
Benjamin T. Bliss - bp 1857
Asa L. Maxson - bp 1857
Clinton R. Lewis - bp 1857, dis 1867
Delos Barber - bp 1857
Cyrus Maxson - bp 1857
Henry R. Maxson - bp 1857, dis 1865
Alburtus Maxson - bp 1857
Norman Maxson - bp 1857, rj 1866
Winfield S. Wells - bp 1857, rj 1868
John C. Bullock - bp 1857, rj 1860
Antinett Stetson - bp 1857, rj 1866
M. Elvira Crandall - bp 1857
Emeline Carpenter - bp 1857
Sarah L. Langworthy - bp 1857
Mariah A. Langworthy - bp 1857, dis 1871
Warren Jaques - bp 1857
H. Lucelia Maxson - bp 1857
Addison Burdick - bp 1857, d Rebel prison 1864
Girdin Lane - bp 1857, d Rebel prison 1864
Altana Lane - bp 1857
Sebeus B. Coon - bp 1857
Mandane Barber - bp 1857
Ira B. Crandall - bp 1857, dis 1870
Caroline Deo - bp 1857

Albert White - bp 1857, rj 1866
Electa White - ad 1857, rj 1866
Elvira Tanner - bp 1858
Diantha Hall - bp 1858
Amanda C. Edwards - bp 1858
Adelia Gilbert - b 1858, dis 1863
John Fox - bp 1858
Clinton Wilcox - bp 1858, d Apr 28, 1867
Aurelia F. Boss - bp 1858
J. Albert Brown - bp 1858

p. 15
Eld. Henry P. Green - ad 1858, d Apr 28, 1868
Harriet Sackey - bp 1858
Erastus A. Green - ad 1860
Nancy Green - ad 1860
DeWane D. Babcock - as 1861, dis 1868
D. A. Fairbank - ad 1861, rj 1866
Mary E. Langworthy - ad 1861
Russel Barber - bp 1863
Adelbert Burdick - bp 1865
Marcellus Burdick - bp 1865, dis 1868, rest
Mary Crandall - bp 1865, dis 1868
Lucetta Maxson - bp 1865, dis 1868
Susan Green - bp 1865
Martin P. Boss - bp 1865
Forest M. B. Babcock - bp 1865
Viola Babcock - bp 1865
Sardinia Hall - bp 1865, dis 1870
Albern H. Burdick - bp 1866
Ormie E. Burdick - bp 1866
Rudolphus Burdick - bp 1866
Emma S. Maxson - bp 1866
Mary Bliss - bp 1866
Sarah A. Prindle - bp 1866
Roxana Slade - ad 1866
Harriet Jaques - as 1866
Joel P. Stillman - bp 1866
Emeline A. Langworthy - bp 1866
Lovinia L. Wells - bp 1866
Elmina M. Barber - bp 1866
Caroline Maxson - ad 1866
Ophelia A. Burdick - bp 1866
Frances I. Jordon - bp 1866
Lucinda Slade - bp 1866
Frances E. Crandall - bp 1866
Sarah Coon - bp 1866
William N. Stillman - ad 1866
Martha P. Burdick - ad 1866

Susan J. Stillman - ad 1868
James R. Crandall - ad 1869
Edgar Wells - bp 1870
Harriet Wells - bp 1870
William Wells - bp 1870
Sophronia Maxson - bp 1870
George Case - bp 1870
Herbert Burdick - bp 1870
Florence Lewis - bp 1870
Sherman Wells - bp 1871
Mary Ette Wells - bp 1871
Benjamin C. Buten - bp 1871
Amelia Buten - bp 1871
Arthur Burdick - bp 1871
Oscar Burdick - bp 1871
Arthur N. Carpenter - bp 1871
Walter Crandall - bp 1871
Desdamonia Crandall - bp 1871
DeForest Baxter - bp 1871
Inez Crandall - bp 1871
Viola Prosser - bp 1871
Arlouine Proser - bp 1871
Lizzie Wells - bp 1871
Amy Lachey - bp 1871
Frank Barber - bp 1871
Gordon Bland - bp 1871
Willie Burdick - bp 1871
Ellen Stillman - bp 1871
Ida Crandall - bp 1871
Edwin S. Foster - bp 1871
Welcome R. Maxson - bp 1871
Biol G. Coon - bp 1871
Fora Hall - bp 1871
Comfort Kenyon - ad 1871
Morton Crandall - ad 1871
DeFrance Coon - ad 1871

p. 17
Mary Lackey - bp 1871
Hattie Jaques - bp 1871
Eliza B. Crandall - bp 1871
May Boss - bp 1871
Adda Witter - bp 1871
Rosena Coon - bp 1871
Joseph D. Stillman - bp 1871
Everett Burdick - bp 1871
Francis Wells - bp 1871
Frank Maxson - bp 1871

Horace Thayer - bp 1871
Jesse Burdick - bp 1871
Andrew Willard - bp 1871
Emmet Witter - bp 1871
Fremont Ennis - bp 1871
Warren Willard - bp 1871
Willie Petit - bp 1871
Mary G. Robinson - bp 1871
Horace Collins - bp 1871

Cassius Maxson - bp 1871
Marcus Slade - bp 1871
Charles Freeman - bp 1871
Walter Bliss - bp 1871
Lucretia Langworthy - bp 1871
Josephine Tierman - bp 1871
Lavinia Green - bp 1871
Ellis A. Witter - ad 1871
Eliza J. Coon - bp 1871

First Genesee SDB Record Book 1827-1871
In possession of town clerk at Little Genesee NY

Second Book
First Genesee Record Book 1871-1926

p. 9
Almond Fairbanks - ad 1871, rj 1877
Emily Cummings - ad 1872
George Cummings - ad 1872, d Jul 23, 1902
Daniel W. Hulett - ad 1873, d 1917
Belle Witter - ad 1874, dis 1875
Andrew Cummings - bp 1874, rj 1902
Laura A. Tanner Maxson - ad 1874, d
Elijah P. Lewis - ad 1876, d Jul 18, 1905
Asenith Lewis - ad 1876, d Mar 3, 1877
Daniel Weyman - bp 1878, d Feb 27, 1879
Ruth E. Weyman - bp 1878, rj 1903
Lillian Witter - bp 1878, dis 1889
Mary A. Burdick - bp 1878, dis 1909
Fred E. Stillman - ad 1878, dis 1905
Mary Jennison - bp 1878, dis 1900
Morton S. Wardner - ad 1878, dis 1882
Sarah L. Wardner - ad 1878, dis 1882
Francis Elliott - bp 1878. d Jun 9, 1887
Cora Stillman - bp 1878, dis 1887
Minnie Green Crandall - bp 1878, dis 1905
Mary C. Burdick - bp 1878, dis 1893
Ida Coon - bp 1878
Albert C. Sanford - bp 1878
Fred L. Burdick - bp 1878, d Oct 15, 1878
Aggie L. Burdick - bp 1878
Maud Crandall Hendrix - bp 1878
Mary E. Bowler - bp 1878
George Boss - bp 1878, dis 1889
Leroy Carpenter - bp 1878, rj 1882
Willie Foster - bp 1878, rj 1900

Lizzie D. Burdick - bp 1878, d Apr 27, 1884
Julia E. Crandall Wakely - bp 1878,
   d Aug 23, 1910
Willard Joy - bp 1878, rj 1883
p. 10
Elizabeth Joy - bp 1878, rj 1883
Rena Coon Stillman - bp 1878, dis 1881
Alice Green Prindle - bp 1878
Florence Green Ayers - bp 1878, dis 1895
Ann F. Colgrove - bp 1878, d Apr 18, 1918
Frank Stillman - bp 1878, dis 1893
Frank Prindle - bp 1878, rj 1882
Herbert Kenyon - bp 1878, d Oct 5, 1887
Orville P. Dana - bp 1878, dis 1905
Lena Foster Ensworth - bp 1878
Emma Fugan - bp 1878, rj 1900
Frank Witter - bp 1878, rj 1882
Fernando C. Lewis - bp 1878, d Jun 12, 1880
Clarence Lewis - bp 1878, rj May 1, 1903
Arthur L. Case - bp 1878, rj 1902
Cortland J. Maxson - bp 1878, d Oct 4, 1823
Thomas G. Crandall - bp 1878, d Oct 10, 1907
Hannah Crandall - bp 1878, d Oct 26, 1919
Minnie J. Green - bp 1878, dis 1890
Elnora A. Hall Loomis - bp 1878, d Mar 16, 1826
Margaret Ennis Stout - bp 1878, rj 1902
John Sanford - bp 1878, rj 1902
Cortland Jaques - bp 1878, rj 1882
Henry Reed - bp 1878
Velina Reed - bp 1878, d Mar 30, 1916
Ida Brown Case - bp 1878

Ettie Brown Slade - bp 1878
John Howe - bp 1878, rj Apr 27, 1883
Mary C. Lewis Millard - ad 1878
Selina Sanford - ad 1878, d Apr 18, 1920
Charles L. Bullock - bp 1878, never joined
Ida Howe Gale - 1878, rj 1907
Ella M. Burdick - bp 1879, dis 1910
Almeda Burdick - ad 1879, d Apr 1, Apr 1891
Lewis Berry - ad 1882, dis 1883
Samuel Howe - bp 1882, dis 1886
George W. Burdick - ad 1883, dis 1893
Minnie W. Burdick - ad 1883, dis 1893
p. 11
Carrie Bliss Woodin - bp 1883
Caoline D. Maxson - ad 1884, d May 29, 1912
H. Benson Clark - ad 1884, d Feb 16, 1924
Flora Clark - ad 1884
Hannah R. Jaques - ad 1884, d Mar 22, 1900
Palermo Lackey - ad 1884, d mar 30, 1897
Maggie Burdick - bp 1884, d Aug 21, 1895
Leone Coon Wilbur - bp 1884
R. Blinn Clark - ad 1885, rj 1902
Jane Burdick - ad 1885, d Mar 12, 1897
L. A. Slike Hutchinson - ad 1885
Ida Slade - ad 1885
Bernice Slike - bp 1885, dis 1898
Nettie Wells - bp 1885
Myrtie Davie Langworthy - bp 1885
Sarah Foster Severson - bp 1885, rj 1908
Josie Crandall Langworthy - bp 1885
Allie Crandall - bp 1885
Horace Hulett - bp 1885
Charles Slade - bp 1885, d Nov 1926
Eva Coon Burdick - bp 1885
Stella Buten Lewis - bp 1885, d Apr 1, 1913
Rose Maxson - bp 1885, d Apr 19, 1908
Emily Wells - ad 1885, d Nov 18, 1916
Mary Edmonds - bp 1886, d Mar 17, 1911
Mary E. Maxson Bell - bp 1886
Alice E. Young Babcock - bp 1886, dis 1894
Merton Burdick - bp 1886, dis 1893
Caroline Jaques - bp 1886, d Mar 9, 1906
Cortland Jaques - bp 1886, rest
Anna Slike - bp 1883, d Mar 24, 1895
Cornelia A. Prosser - ad 1887, d Oct 27, 1907
Julia A. Jordan - bp 1887

Lois Jaques - bp 1887
Delany Bently Fairbanks - bp 1887
Mary Case Fairchild - bp 1887
Lafayette Gibbs - bp 1887, rj 1900
Mary Ida Gibbs - bp 1887, d Jul 5, 1888
p. 12
Lydia A. Millard - ad 1887, d Jul 18, 1926
Fannie Davis Burdick - ad 1887, dis 1905
Lester Clark - bp 1888
Hattie Jaques - bp 1888, d May 4, 1897
Harriet E. A. Crandall - ad 1889, dis 1891
Elvira Crandall - ad 1890, rj 1900
Newton Burdick - bp 1890, rj 1902
Frederick Perkins - bp 1890, rj 1900
Thomas B. Burdick - bp 1890
Leslie Bliss - bp 1890
Fred Burdick - bp 1890
Harvey Burdick - bp 1890, dis 1893
Mathew Coon - ad 1890, dis 1913
Nancy Stone - ad 1890, d Mar 27, 1899
Eva Spencer - bp 1890, rj
Sherman Perry - bp 1890, rj 1902
Aaron DeGroff - bp 1890, rj 1900
Harriet Perkins - bp 1890, dis 1900
Myra Slocum Cooper - bp 1890, d Jun 1907
Adelbert Coon - bp 1890
Vina Clark Bliss - bp 1890
Sarah Worden - ad 1891, d Aug 28, 1900
Samuel Howe - ad 1891, d Jul 27, 1892
Mary Howe - ad 1891, d Jun 7, 1897
Frank Witter - bp 1891, dis 1891
Nellie Fay Carpenter - bp 1892, rj 1902
Edna Hall - bp 1892
Leola Slade - bp 1892
Lena Slade - bp 1892, rj 1902
Beth Sanford Farley - bp 1892, dis 1902
Amy Sanford Crandall - bp 1892
Nina Crandall - bp 1892, rj 1903
Katie Willard - bp 1892
Winona Champlin Kenyon - bp 1892, dis 1907
Ada Reynolds - bp 1892, rj 1889
p. 13
Edna Pettite Millard - bp 1892, dis 1920
Josephine Pettite - ad 1892
Fanny Pettite Lewis - ad 1892
Fanny A. Lanphere - ad 1892, dis 1895
Lydia Bennehoff - ad 1892, d Mar 28, 1922

Emerson W. Ayers - ad 1893, dis 1895
Eva A. Slade - bp 1893
Corine Smith - bp 1893
Mary Willard Steven - bp 1893
Virgil Clark - bp 1893, dis 1925
Benjamin F. Green - bp 1893, d Apr 24, 1898
Martha Green - bp 1893, d Jul 2, 1923
Lizzie Burdick Lions - bp 1893
Sylvester S. Powell - bp 1893, rj 1898
Sarah E. Powell - bp 1893, rj 1898
Eliza Kenyon - bp 1893, d Dec 31, 1897
Mary A. Collins - bp 1893
Benjamin Wilbur - bp 1893
Frank Preston - bp 1893, rj 1902
Charles W. Fairbanks - bp 1893, rj 1902
Leander W. Lewis - bp 1893, d Dec 6, 1900
Elbert C. Smith - ad 1893
Carrie E. Crandall - ad 1893, d Apr 5, 1814
Judson Dana - bp 1893
Josephine N. Coon Hiscock - bp 1893
Bertha Buten Champlin - bp 1893,
   d Dec 18, 1909
Earle Crandall - bp 1893
J. H. Backus - ad 1893, rj 1907
Fanny Backus - ad 1893
Albert W. Crandall - ad 1893, d Aug 30, 1901
Hattie E. A. Crandall - ad 1893,
   d Jan 28, 1897
Aroa A. Stillman Bristol - bp 1894
Charles E. Saunders - ad 1894
Mary C. Saunders - ad 1894, d Jul 6, 1894
Lewis Champlin - bp 1894
Menzo Lanphere - ad 1896, dis 1913
Fannie A. Lanphere - ad 1896, dis 1913
Ethel Crandall Monroe - bp 1896

p. 14
Roy A. Farley - ad 1896, dis 1902
Irene Post Hulett - ad 1896
Mary Lewis - bp 1896
Clayton L. Lewis - bp 1896
Frederick F. Lewis - bp 1896
Earle Pettite - bp 1898
Delos Jaques - bp 1898
Norman Baxter - bp 1898, rj 1903
Lizzie Hazard - bp 1898, rj 1903
Laura Sanford - bp 1898, d Apr 21, 1918
Anna Crandall - bp 1898
Stella Jaques - bp 1898
Donna Jaques DePew - bp 1896

Flora Slade - bp 1898
Ethel Slade - bp 1898
Miriam G. Powell - bp 1898, rj 1898
Rev. E. Burdett Coon - ad 1899, dis 1904
Cordelia E. Coon - ad 1899, dis 1904
Sylvester Powell - ad 1900, dis 1902
Sarah E. Powell - ad 1900, dis 1902
Miriam G. Powell - ad 1900, dis 1902
Olive Dana - ad 1900, dis 1905
Olive M. Powell - bp 1901, dis 1902
Paul R. Powell - bp 1901, dis 1902
Mary L. Burdick - bp 1902
L Harold Burdick - bp 1902
Lucian T. Burdick - bp 1902
Philip C. Burdick - bp 1902
Paul S. Burdick - bp 1902, dis 1918
Frank E. Burdick - bp 1902
Guy M. Burdick - bp 1902, d Nov 29, 1918
Herman R. Burdick - bp 1902
Elmer G. Burdick - bp 1902
Leon M. Burdick - bp 1902
Raymond C. Burdick - bp 1902
Charles M. Hazzard - bp 1902
Claude Conser - bp 1902, rj 1908
Reva L. Pettite - bp 1902, dis 1909
Mildred I. Slade - bp 1902
Edwin A. Gibbs - ad 1902, rj 1906
Sherman Green - ad 1902
Harry E. Stebbins - bp 1902, d Feb 9, 1920
Leonard S. Gibbs - bp 1902, rj 1907
Cora F. Gibbs - bp 1902, rj 1907
Eva Crandall - bp 1902, dis 1905
Vina Burdick - ad 1902
S. H. Babcock - ad 1904, dis 1910
Elizabeth Babcock - ad 1904, dis 1910
J. L. Hull - ad 1904
Minnie B. Hall - ad 1904
Lucy C. Green - bp 1905
Andrew Willard - bp 1905, d Aug 17, 1920
Myrtle M. Hall - bp 1906, d Jan 19, 1913
Mary Alzina Lanphere Burdick - bp 1906
Ann M. Clark - bp 1906
Lou E. Smith Burdick - bp 1906
Jesse Clarke - ad 1906, dis 1915
Viola Clarke - bp 1906, dis 1915
Dudley P. Hall - bp 1906
Leo S. Lanphere - ad 1907, d Mar 1, 1923

Jesse A. Burdick - bp 1907, dis 1909
Edith J. Burdick - bp 1907, dis 1909
Dora Slade Baxter - bp 1907
Hortense Fairbank Burdick - bp 1907
Mildred Fairbank White - bp 1907
Rena Woolhizer - ad 1907
Ethel Clarke - bp 1907, dis 1915
*Mark R. Sanford - bp 1907
Edna Stebbins -bp 1907, d Aug 10, 1919
Melpha Connor - bp 1907
Oral Connor Reeland, -bp 1907

Julia Baxter - bp 1907
Zell D. Perry - bp 1907, d Mar 28, 1918
Lillian Baxter - bp 1907, rj 1918
Lucian M. Bristol - bp 1907, d Oct 23, 1924
William D. Clarke - ad 1917, dis 1910
T. Edgar Green - ad 1907
Mahala Green - ad 1907, d Apr 7, 1913
Hiram Grow - ad 1908
Vernon E. Stevens - ad 1909
Walter H. Burdick - bp 1910

*Dea. Mark Rowland Sanford - bp 1907; lay pastor
Deaconess Edna Bliss Burdick Sanford - ad 1922
Rev. Don Alberne Sanford - b. Jan 14, 1926, bp 1934, pastor, writer,
teacher, historian   (listed in later records)

**Second Book of Records
First Genesee SDB Church 1871-1926
In possession of town clerk**

Second Genesee SDB Church
Oswayo Creek, Portville Twsp., Cattaragus Co. NY
Also called Oswayo
First organization 1834-1862

Constituent Members 1834

- Enoch K. Maxson
- W. P. Stillman
- Daniel Bliven
- Robert Stillman
- Albert M. Burdick
- Samuel A. Barber
- L. F. Maxson
- Palermo Lackey
- Benjamin C. Maxson
- Benjamin C. Maxson Jr
- George S. Crandall
- Henry Smith
- Avery Palmer
- Sheffield Main
- Prentice Main
- Luke Coon
- Zacheus Maxson
- Rufus Cole
- Lauriett Maxson
- Mary Ann Stillman
- Polly Palmer
- Fanny (?) Bliven
- Emily H. Main
- Polly Ann Main
- Hannah Main
- Syntha E. Burdick
- Nancy Barber
- Patty Maxson
- Susan Smith
- Nancy Palmer
- Prudence Crandall
- Harriet Cole
- Mary Smith

Petition to be set off from First Genesee 1843
MS19x.216
CRR vault

Second Genesee SDB Church NY
Reorganized as Portville 1862-c1934
Located at Main Settlement, Portville Twsp., Cattaragus Co. NY
No primary records extant

Third Genesee SDB Church 1835-1843
Dodge's Creek, Genesee Twsp., Allegany Co. NY
Also called Dodge's Creek. No primary records extant

Reorganized as West Genesee 1843-c1908

Constituent Members

p.3
Edwin M. Crandall -- ad 1843, dis
John Saunders - bp 1843
Ethan P. Crandall - ad 1843
Orenzo Coon - ad 1843, excom 1846
Lindon Cradnall Jr - ad 1843, d
Electa Crandall - ad 1843

Cornelia A. Crandall - ad 1843
Betsey Smith - ad 1843, d Mar 19, 1863
Hannah Childs - ad 1843, d
Sally Coon - ad 1834, dis, d
Narcissa L. Crandall - ad 1843, excom 1845
Jane Reed - ad 1843, excom 1845

Members

p. 14
David C. Gardner - ad 1843
Betsey Nye - ad 1843, d
Elliot Smith - ad 1845, rj 1853
Rachel Maxson - ad 1846
Ann Hyde - ad 1846
Charles Sisson - ad 1846, dis

p. 16
Jane Reed - ad 1845, excom
Orenzo Coon - ad 1846, excom
Almond Fairbanks - ad 1846, excom

Persons admitted from other churches

p. 17
John I. Brown - ad 1843 fr Persia, d Nov. 28, 1862
Fidelia Brown - ad 1843, fr Persia NY, d
Sarah Gardner - ad 1843 fr First Genesee, d
Lorenzo D. Ayres - ad 1843 fr DeRuyter, dis
Lucy M. Ayres - ad 1843 fr Clarence, dis 1851
Lurania Noise - ad 1844 fr Free Will Baptist Church of Hume
Daniel Childs - ad 1844 fr Free Will Baptist Church of Hume, d
Demaruis Coon - ad 1844 fr 2nd Brookfield dis
Samuel Yapp - ad 1844, fr Friendship, d Aug 1, 1864
Mary Yapp - ad 1844 fr Friendship Church, d Aug 23, 1864
Susan H. Yapp - ad 1844 fr First Baptist Church in Olean
Abigail M. Yapp - ad 1844 fr First Baptist Church in Olean
Eliza M. Yapp - ad 1844 fr First Baptist Church in Olean, d
Henry C. Champlin - ad 1844 fr First Alfred
Polly Coon - ad 1845 fr DeRuyter NY, dis
James C. Brown - ad 1846 fr Friendship Church
Sally Brown - ad 1846 fr Third Brookfield NY
Almond Fairbanks - bp 1846 in West Almond excom.
Eleanor F. Fairbanks - bp 1846 in West Almond rj 1852
Eld. H. P. Green - ad 1848 fr First Genesee NY,
Mary A. Irish - ad 1849 fr First Alfred NY
John Noise - ad 1850 fr Free Will Baptist Church
Emily Baker - ad 1850 fr Clarence
Daniel B. Crandall - ad 1850 fr First Genesee NY

Members in 1852

p. 18
Samuel H. Crandall - bp 1846
Juliett L. Payne - bp 1846
Mary A. Payne - bp 1846, rj 1851
Samuel Henry Smith - bp 1846, dp by request 1852
Charles D. Coon - bp 1846, dis
John J. Smith - bp 1846
Harriet Crandall - bp 1846
Fanny Baker - bp 1846

p. 19
Edwin M. Crandall - dis
John Saunders
Ethan P. Crandall
David C. Gardner - dis to Friendship, 1860
Elliott Smith - rj 1853
Charles Sisson - dis
John J. Brown - d Nov 28, 1862
Samuel Yapp - dis
James C. Brown - dis
Samuel H. Crandall
John J Smith
Eld. Henry P. Green
John Nois
Daniel B. Crandall
Albert H. Crandall - bp 1852
John M. Crandall - d Sep 1864
John Sanford - rj 1869
Olson Crandall - dis 1854
Ray C. Smith - rj 1854
William Cranson - rj 1855

p. 20
David Yapp
Edgar Irish - dis 1866
George R. Brown - d Nov 18, 1862
Ely P. Brown - d Mar 27, 1862
Jasper N. Murry - rj 1854
Albert Crandall - member of old church
Daniel S. Truman - ex 1863
Joseph S. Crandall - dis

Claudius Young - ex
John Champlain - ex
Charles M. Crandall

p. 21
Betsey Smith - d Mar 20, 1863
Sally Coon - dis
Electa Crandall
Cornelia A. Prosser
Narcissa L. Champlin
Betsey Nye - dis, d
Rachel Maxson
Ann Hyde - dis
Lurania Noise - d Jun 15, 1866
Mary Yapp
Susan H. Yapp
Abigail A. Yapp - ex
Eliza Yapp - d 1852
Mary E. Crandall
Juliett L. Payne
Harriet Saunders
Mary S. Irish - ex 1863
Emily Baker - rj 1882
Genette E. Crandall - bp 1852, dis 1864
Louisa E. Maxson

p. 22
Laurett E. Maxson
Jane Maxson - dis 1869
Alnoria Crandall
Alzinia Crandall - dis 1855
Betsey Ann Smith Springer - excom 1865
Fanny Crandall - member of old church
Martha Sanford - d
Lydia Truman - ex 1863
Olive Crandall - dis
Betsey Brown - d
Sarah A. Champlin
Laury Vincent - ex 1864
Eunice Price ? - bp, dis
Alys Malinda Firington - dis 1858

Third Genesee NY SDB Church Records 1843-1853
CRR.2.2 vault
IMS:1995

Third Book (some duplication)
West Genesee (Third Genesee) Membership List
1843 -- 1896

p. 4

Silas Burdick - bp 1857
Pheby Burdick - ad 1857
Mary S. Sanford - ad 1857 fr First Brookfield, excom 1863
Arza Coon - ad 1858 fr DeRuyter
Anna Elisa Coon - ad 1858 fr DeRuyter, dis
Charles Willbur - ad 1858 fr Second Alfred
Harriet Willbur - ad 1858 fr Second Alfred
Ann E. Maxson - ad 1858 fr Second Alfred
George Irish - ad 1858 fr the old church

p. 5

Lavern Burdick - bp 1858
Arlouine E. Coon - bp 1858, dis
Almeda Vincent - bp 1858, ex 1862
Andrew B. Brown - bp 1858, d Sep 22, 1863
Marcus M. Crandall - bp 1858, d Jun 28, 1862
Floid M. Crandall - bp 1858, d Oct 9, 1864
Milo Green - bp 1858, ex
Norten Vincent - bp 1858, ex 1863
Emila Vincent - bp 1858, ex 1863
Adelisa Burdick - bp 1858
S. G. Burdick - bp 1858, dis 1866
Adaresta Crandall - bp 1858, keeps Sunday
Hadwin Irish - bp 1858, d Aug 1864
Wardner Irish - bp 1858, ex Dec 2, 1866
Mary Irish - bp 1858, dis 1866
Marthy Irish - bp 1858, dis 1866
Brittany S. Smith - bp 1858
Joshua Potter - bp 1858, suspended 1864
Sarah Potter - bp 1858, suspended 1864
Mary J. Noyes - bp 1858, excom 1865

p. 6

Welthy Potter - ad 1858 fr First Day Baptist, d May 4, 1860
John Crandall - ad 1858 fr Persia
Eliza Crandall - ad 1858 fr Persia
Lydia Crandall - ad 1858 fr Second Genesee
Abigail Crandall - ad 1852
Rachel Eastman - bp 1858, suspended
Eld. Z. Campbell - ad 1858 fr WI Church, dis
Amy Campbell - ad 1858 fr WI Church, dis
Eld. Cos. A. Burdick - ad 1860 fr Albion WI
Amanda Burdick, formerly Lewis - ad 1861 fr Second Alfred, dis
James Young - ad 1861 fr Independence
Caroline Young - ad 1861 fr Independence
Sidney Keller - bp 1861, excom 1865
Lucy Champlain - bp 1861
Harriet Willber - bp 1861
Rhoda Willber - bp 1861
Ann Vinett Crandall - bp 1861

p. 7

Shefield B. Main - ad 1862, dis
James Main - ad 1862, dis 1862
Malvina Main - ad 1862, dis
Olive Barber - ad 1862
Frances E. Main - dis
Eld. Ray Green - ad 1862, d Mar 1864
Mrs. Ray Green - ad 1862
George J. Crandall - ad 1864 fr Watson NY
Elizabeth A. Crandall - ad 1864 fr Watson NY
Defrance Coon - bp 1865
Adelbert Crandall - bp 1865, keeps Sunday
Lanesia Champlain - bp 1865
Hattie W. Oliver - bp 1865, excom
Adista Coon - bp 1865, dis
Delmina Coon - bp 1865
Amanda Brown - ad 1866 fr Second Alfred
David C. Green - ad 1866 fr Second Alfred
Lovina Green - ad 1866 fr Second Alfred

p. 8   Members 1866

Ethan R. Crandall - d Dec 31, 1877
Electa Crandall - d
John Saunders - d
Harriet Saunders - d
Rachel Maxson - d Mar 16, 1885
John Noyce
Lurania Noyce - d Jun 15, 1866
Albert B. Crandall - d
Fanny Crandall - d
Martha Sanford - d Mar 2, 1877
Sarah Ann Champlin - May 1888
Betsey Brown - d Mar 10, 1867
Cornelia Prosser - dis
Narcissa L. Champlin
Juliett L. Payne
Charles D. Coon - dis
Charles M. Crandall
Abigail Crandall
Lauriett E. Livermore - dp

Members 1866

p. 9
A. K. Crandall - d May 20, 1920
Lovisa E. Crandall - d Jan 10, 1929
John J. Smith
Brittany Smith - d Dec 29, 1893
David E. Yapp
Mary E. Yapp - d
Elnora Crandall - dp
Silas Burdick - bp 1857
Phebe Burdick - bp 1857, d
Charles Willbur - ad 1858 fr Second Alfred, dis 1872
Hannah Willbur - ad 1858 fr Second Alfred, dis 1872
Ann E. Maxson - ad 1858 fr Second Alfred, d Feb 14, 1885
John Crandall - ad 1858 fr Persia
Eliza Crandall - ad 1858 fr Persia, dis 1872
Lydia Crandall - ad 1858 fr Second Genesee, dis 1875
James Young - ad 1861 fr Independence, d
Caroline Young - ad 1861 fr Independence, dis
Mrs. Ray Green - ad 1862 fr Hayfield PA, d
George J. Crandall - ad 1864 fr Watson NY, dis 1868
Elizabeth A. Crandall - ad 1864 fr Watson NY, dis 1868

p. 10
Lavern Burdick - bp 1858, dis 1873
Ada C. Burdick - bp 1858
Adaresta Munger - bp 1858
Wardner Irish - bp 1861, ex 1868
Harriet Willber - bp 1861
Rhoda Willber - bp 1861, dis to Portville 1876
Ann Vinett Crandall - bp 1861
Defrance Coon - bp 1865, dis 1870
Adelbert Crandall - bp 1865
Louisa Champlin - bp 1865, ex 1868
Hattie W. Oliver - bp 1865, ex 1867
Adista Coon - bp 1865, dis 1870
Delmina Coon - bp 1865, dis 1873
Amanda Brown - bp 1865, ex 1867
David C. Green - ad 1866 fr Second Alfred, dis
Lavina Green - ad 1866 fr Second Alfred, dis
Emily L. Cummings - ad 1867 fr Portville, dis 1872
Eugene R. Burdick - ad 1866, dis 1872
Francelia Burdick - bp 1866, dis 1872

p. 11
Eld. Stephen Burdick - ad 1869, dis 1872
Susan M. Burdick - ad 1869, dis 1872
Weltha Sanford - bp 1871, dp
James C. Brown - ad 1869, d
Mary Sanford - ad 1869, dp
Clarke Green - bp 1871, dis
Ida Green - bp 1871, dis
Herbert Yapp - bp 1871, dis
Wardner Irish - ad 1873, dis
Alfred Antisdale - ad 1873
Byron E. Maxson - bp 1873, dis
Emley E. Coon - bp 1873, dp 1888
Evangeline Antisdale - bp 1873
Vesta Antisdale - bp 1873
Samuel H. Crandall - ad 1873, dis
Alzina Crandall - ad 1873 fr Christiana WI, dis
Estella G. Keller - ad 1873, dis
Minor Walton - bp 1873, dis
Ann Jane Walton - bp 1873, dis
Mary Irish - rest 1873, d

p. 12
I. J. Lewis - ad 1873, excom 1888
Ella Lewis - ad 1873
Sarah A. Lewis - ad 1873
Carrie I. Lewis - ad 1873
Lorenzo Prince - bp 1873, ex 1879
Lucy Prince - bp 1873, ex 1879
Martha Sanford - bp 1873, ex
Nathan A. Childs - bp 1874
Marion L. Keller - bp 1874, dis
Mary A. Lewis - bp 1874, dp
Weltha O. Crandall - bp 1874, dis
Rachel M. Sanford - bp 1874, d
F. Dennyn Crandall - ad 1874 fr Friendship Church
Bro. A. G. Crofoot - ad 1878, dis
Sister E. G. Crofoot - ad 1878, dis
Bro. F. Gardner - ad 1878, dp 1884
Bro. Edwin Howard - ad 1877 fr Portville Church

p. 13
Libbie E. Maxson - ad 1878, dis
Annie Lamm - bp 1878
James H. Crandall - ad 1879 fr Brookfield
Ordelia O. Crandall - ad 1879 fr Brookfield
Minnie M. Crandall - ad 1879
George P. Kenyon - ad 1879 fr First Alfred, dis
Mary M. Kenyon - ad 1879 fr First Hebron, dis
Fannie Walton - bp 1879, dp

Amos Kenyon - ad 1881, d
Sally Kenyon - ad 1881
Asa Antisdall - bp 1881
Susan Walton - bp 1881, dis
E. A. Witter - ad 1885 fr Andover Church
Mary Benjamin Witter - ad 1885 fr Andover Church

Sarah Worden - bp 1885, dis
Alvira Keller - ad 1885, dis 1895
p. 14
Elsie Crandall - bp 1892, dis
I. T. Lewis - dis, rest 1896

CRR 1959.2.4 vault
Third Genesee SDB Church Records 1843-1863
IMS:1995

Little Rhode Island Cemetery Burials
Genesee Twsp., Allegany Co. NY

"The Little Rhode Island Cemetery is located at the Junction of Hibbard St. and County Road #5 in Genesee Twsp., Allegany NY. It received its name from the fact that most of the burials consist of township pioneers who came from RI, together with many of their children who died at a young age from the rigors and diseases of that period. There are no known cemetery association records, maps or other records for burials until after 1900, and it is presumed that numerous interments occurred without gravestones to identify the deceased.

About 1975 the then county historian provided two CETA workers to list data from gravestones of this burial ground. Due to illegibility of numerous gravestones, the complete accuracy was almost impossible, although names of the people seemed to be no problem.

The following is a composite reconstruction using the CETA record, the Burdick, Greene, Maxson, and Potter genealogies, Beer's and Minard's county histories, census records, *The Bolivar Breeze*, and *The Sabbath Recorder.*

The accuracy of this composite is, therefore, only as accurate as the sources from which the data was taken."

Babcock, Alanson Abel - s/o Peleg Jr. & Lucinda, no gravestone, d Jan 20, 1841
Babcock, Lucinda - w/o Peleg Babcock, Jr, b 1804, d Feb 2, 1840
Bliss, David C. - b Jan 5, 1841 Newport RI, d Feb 11, 1891
Bliss, Ebenezer David - s/o Thomas Ward & Martha Boss, m Sarah C. Thurston, b Dec 29, 1796 Newport RI, d Aug 1, 1884
Bliss, Eliza E. - b Sep 30, 1821 Newport RI, d Oct 17, 1886
Bliss, Martha Boss - w/o Ebenezer D., b Nov 20, 1797 Newport RI, d Aug 1, 1884
Bliss, William D. - s/o Ebenezer D., b Mar 26, 1838, d Jun 28, 1862 near Richmond VA; 4th Sgt Co. I, 27th Reg. NYS Vols., Union Color Bearer

p. 2

Boone (or Boane), Aurilla (or Orilla) L. Fairbanks - d/o Danforth A. & Melissa Coon Fairbanks, b Feb 29, 1856, d Dec 31, 1885
Bowler, Mary L. - d/o William L. & Eliza F. Ennis, d Sep 7, 1846, one yr
Burdick, Catherine L. - d/o Jabez & Mary Jaques, b Jul 22, 1834 Little Genesee, d Feb 18, 1856
Burdick, Delila P. - d/o Jabez & Mary A., b 1843 Genesee Twsp., d May 24, 1847
Burdick, Electra P. - w/o Ira J., b Jun 13, 1828
Burdick, Elizabeth Whitford - b 1757, d Feb 22, 1856, 100 yrs
Burdick, George W. - s/o Jabez & Mary A., b Nov 5, 1850, d Dec 9, 1935
Burdick, Ira - s/o Jabez & Elizabeth Whitford, b 1798 prob Berlin NY, d Jan 5, 1827, m Polly Wilcox
Burdick, Jabez - d Jan 1, 1854, m Mary Jane Jaques (1811-1911)
Burdick, Mary Adeline - d/o Jabez & Mary A., b 1838 Genesee Twsp., d Feb 6, 1881
Burdick, Mary Ann Jaques - d/o Samuel & Sarah Webster Jaques, b May 22, 1811 Rockville RI, d Nov 28, 1911, 100 yrs
Burdick, Polly Wilcox - d/o Job Wilcox, w/o Ira Burdick, b Jan 1803, d Aug 4, 1861
Burdick, Samantha Ann Parker - d/o Isaac N. & Sarah Ann Bennett Parker Parker, w/o Hiram Benton Burdick, b Oct 1839 Portville Cattaraugus Co, NY, d Jul 13, 1866

p. 3

Colegrove, Avis Hall - d Jun 9, 1851, m Amos Colegrove Jan 18, 1851
Coon, D. L. - d Jan 2, 1879, 32 yrs, 3 mo
Coon, Rowland - b Mar 17, 1791 Hopkinton RI, d Mar 19, 1848
Coon, Sally - w/o Rowland, b 1791 prob RI, d Nov 25, 1963
Cooper, Adelbert - b 1884, d Jan 10, 1910
Crandall, Amy K. Lackey - d/o Palermo & Eunice Edwards Lackey, b Jan 11, 1839 Genesee Twsp., d Jan 25, 1925, m James A. Bond, m Ezekiel Rogers Crandall
Crandall, Henry Edwin (Eddie) - s/o Morton D. & Sarah Bliss, b Oct 12, 1857 Scio, d Jan 20, 1858

Crandall, Ezekiel E. - s/o of Phineas & Ruth Rogers, b Sep 7, 1873 Hopkinton RI, d Jul 15, 1855,
    m Susan Wells (1789-1861)

Crandall, Ezekiel Rogers - s/o Ezekiel & Susan Wells, b Jun 26, 1820
    Hophinton RI, d Mar 20, 1915, m Nancy Celestia, m 2nd Mrs. Amy K. Lackey Bond (Mrs. James)

Crandall, Martha Alice ("Mattie A.") - d/o Morton D. & Sarah Bliss
    b Dec 31, 1859, d May 7, 1863

Crandall, Mary Adeline - d/o Morton D. & Sara Bliss, b Dec 16, 1861, d Jun 16, 1875

p. 4

Crandall, Nancy Celestia Burdick - d/o Ira & Polly Wilcox Burdick, b Dec 27, 1825, d Nov 14, 1878,
    m Ezekiel Rogers Crandall (1820-1915

Crandall, Susan Wells - d/o Samuel &. Susan Potter Wells, b Nov. 14, 1789 Hopkinton RI,
    d Apr 29, 1861, m Ezekiel E. Crandall

Cottrell (or Cuttrell), Nancy - b 1787, d Jun 20, 1848, m Abel Cottrell

Cummings, Walter W. - d Jul 1882, 24 yrs, m Alice Green(e)

Dickerson, Mary - d Nov 17, 1885, 67 yrs

Fairbanks, Charles L. - s/o Ephaiim & Phoebe L., d Sep 6, 1861 6yrs-7mo-7da

Fairbanks, Delmont Elroy - s/o Danforth & Melissa C., b Apr 13, 1851, d May 24, 1859

Fairbanks, Melissa D. Coon - d Dec 1, 1860, 2nd w/o Danforth A. Fairbanks

Gardner, Sarah R. Greene - d/o Amos & Esther Lewis Gardner, d Dec 15, 1849, 28yrs-2mo-8da,
    w/o David C. Gardner

Gibbs, Fanny - d/o William & Eleanor Maxson Bliven, b Aug 1772 Westerly RI,
    d Feb 2, 1854 82 yrs-2 da, m Pardon Greene (1769-1799), m Nathan Stillman, Israel Gibbs

Green, Amos - s/o Benjamin & Frances G. Rogers, b Feb 25, 1792 Hophinton RI, d Mar 25, 1885,
    m Esther Lewis

p. 5

Green, Clark - s/o William Bliven & Mary Hiscox Green, b Oct 10, 1819 RI, d Mar 30, 1837,
    killed by falling tree limb

Green, Edna - d/o Henry D. & Sarah C., d Feb 17, 1867

Green, Esther Lewis - d/o David Lewis, b 1790, d Dec 13, 1862, w/o Amos Green(e) (1792-1885)

Green, Frances Rogers - d/o Matthew & Esther Rogers, d Sep 30, 1852, 1st w/o Benjamin F. Green
    (1825-1898)

Greene, Rev. Henry Parks - s/o Benjamin & Frances Rogers, b Mar 28, 1798 Hopkinton RI,
    d Apr 28, 1868, m Lucy Rogers

Greene, Ida Eugenia - d/o Henry D. & Sarah Green(e), b 1860, d Jun 20, 1868

Greene, Lucy Rogers, d/o Ephraim & Hannah Rogers, b Aug 6, 1801, Waterford CT, d May 9, 1846,
    w/o Rev. Henry Parks Greene

Green(e), Mary Jane, d/o Henry P. & Lucy Rogers Rogers, b May 25, 1836, d Sep 25, 1852

Hall, Perry, s/o Benjamin & Wealthy, d May 23, 1845 Sharon, Potter Co. PA, 23 yrs-9mo-21da

Hall, Wealthy - b Jan 27, 1792, d May 16, 1880, m W. H. (Benjamin?) Hill, Lois M. - b 1834, d 1884

p. 6

Hornblower, Lucy Esther Greene - d/o Amos & Esther Lewis Greene, b 1817 RI, d Nov 23, 1842
    Ceres Twsp. PA, m William E. Hornblower

Hornblower, William Lucas - s/o William & Lucy Green, d Dec 21, 1842

Hulbert, Eugene D. - d Feb 7, 1947, 67 yrs-8mo-15da, m Mary Minerva ???

Hulbert, Mary Minerva, b 1887, d Jan 8, 1968, m Eugene D. Hulbert

Irish, Maria E. - d/o Benjamin & Elizabeth Greene Potter, b Sep 20, 1810 Hopkinton RI,
    d Oct 3, 1844, w/o George Irish Jr

Jaques, Asa H. - s/o Samuel & Sarah Webster, b Nov 27, 1826 Rockville RI, d Jul 25, 1915,
    m Harriet Stillman

Jaques, Harriet - b Sep 12, 1827, d May 12, 1886, w/o Asa H. Jaques

Jaques, Mary L. - d/o Asa H. & Harriet S., b 1850, d Dec 6, 1860, 9 yrs

Jaques, Samuel - b 1787 Rockville RI, d Mar 4, 1883, m Sarah Webster

Jacques, Sarah Angelica - d/o Asa H. & harriet S., b 1855, d Nov 1, 1861, 5 yrs-10mo-12d

Jacques, Sarah - d Nov 21, 1874, 84 yrs w/o Samuel Jaques

p. 7

Langworthy, Asa - s/o John A., b May 4, 1782, d Aug 22, 1868 Portville, Cattaraugus Co. NY,
    m Ruth Crandall d/o Philip & Margaret Frye Crandall

Langworthy, Edwin Philip - s/o Asa & Ruth C., b Oct 2, 1821, d May 31, 1850 Wirt, Allgany Co. NY

Langworthy, Emma Maria - d/o Asa & Ruth C. Langworthy, b Jul 6, 1837, d Feb 3, 1837

Langworthy, Ira - d Jan 28, 1817

Langworthy, Orville Everett - s/o Asa & Emma, d Mar 3, 1841, 14mo-3da

Langworthy, Ruth A. Crandall, d/o Philip & Margaret Frye Crandall, b Sep 9, 1795 Newport RI,
    d May 1, 1863 Friendship, Allegany Co. NY

Langworthy, Sanford - s/o Asa & Ruth C., b Sep 30, 1834, d May 2, 1840/41

Langworthy, Thomas Wayland - s/o Asa & Emma, d Dec 4, 1842 Alfred NY

Lewis, Fernando C. - b Nov 12, 1845, d Jun 12, 1880, m Mary Cornelia Smith
    d/o Julius & Sarah Ann Morse Smith

Lewis, Merville E.- s/o Leander W. & Clarissa Worden, d Feb 28, 1840

Maxson, Asa Lyman - s/o Joel & Mercy Green,, b Oct 9, 1832, d Apr 24, 1915,
    m Abby Caroline Johnson d/o Ezekiel & Abby Wilbur Johnson,
    m 2nd Mrs. Caroline Babcock Young d/o Ichabod & Sally Babcock wid/o James Young

p. 8

Maxson, Caroline A. Johnson - d/o Ezekiel & Abby Johnson, b 1838, d Aug 19, 1881, 43 yrs-1mo-24,
    w/o Asa Maxson

Maxson, Lydia Potter - d/o George & Content Maxson Potter, b Oct 10, 1766 Hopkinton RI,
    d Jun 15, 1842, w/o Joseph Maxson (1771-1856)

McKelvey, Maude Hewitt - d/o Benjamin Hewitt, d Sep 16, 1908 West Clarksville, NY,
    w/o Laverne McKelvey

Merritt, Benjamin C. - b Jan 25, 1821, d Aug 23, 1885, m 1st Sarah Edwards, m 2nd Phebe Eliza
    Barber

Merritt, Betsey Stevens - b 1821, d Jan 5, 1867, m Amos C. Merritt Alfred 22, 1846 Alfred NY

Merritt, Florence A. - d/o Benjamin & Sarah Edwards, d Jan 9, 1857, 2 yrs-3mo-3da

Meritt, James M. W. - s/o George & Lucy Lewis - b Jan 4, 1835, d Sep 3, 1920

Merritt, Llewellyn S. - adopt s/o Amos & Betsey, b 1850, d Oct 7, 1861

Potter, Fanny S. Green - d/o Luther & Susan Merritt Green, b Jun 18, 1819,
    d Aug 4, 1888 Independence NY, w/o George Potter, no children

Potter, Dea. George Potter Jr, s/o George & Betsey Rogers Potter, b Nov 2, 1811 Westerly RI,
    d Mar 26, 1856, m Fanny S. Green Mar 11, 1841

p. 9

Potter, Mary - d/o George Sr & Betsey Rogers, b 1812, d Oct 9, 1840

Potter, Sarah Fenner - d/o Benjamin & Elizabeth Fenner, b 1818, d Feb 11, 1840

Rogers, Dana Marccellus - s/o Henry C. & Sara A., d Oct 1, 1852, 2 yrs-2mo

Rogers, Elizabeth F. - d/o Ephraim A. & Chloe d May 31, 1827, 14 yrs-2mo

Rogers, Emily E. d/o Matthew & Esther Greene, d May 18, 1847

Rogers, Emily Minette - d/o Henry C. & Sarah A. Rogers, d Oct 4, 1852, 11 mo-16 da

Rogers, Ephraim - d Mar 2, 1842, 62 yrs

Rogers, Lydia Stillman - d/o Maxson Stillman, d May 18, 1845 Wirt Twsp, Allgany Co., w/o Clark
    Rogers

Ross, Frank - G. A. R. 1861-1865 Civil War veteran - b Nov 5, 1852, d Jun 2, 1886

Sanford, Martha - d Mar 21, 1886, w/o R. S. Sanford

Sanford, R. S. - d Aug 20, 1850, m Martha

Sanford, Richard C. - d May 20, 1850, 49 yrs

Scott, Arthur W. - s/o A. R. & L. M. Scott, b 1857, d Apr 7, 1858

Scott Horace L. - s/o A. R. & L.M., b 1859, d Aug 26, 1863

Scott, William E. - s/o A. R. & L. M., b 1862, d Mar 5, 1862

Shotts, Anna - wid /o Kie Shotts, d 1941, lived in Clarion Co. PA until 1936

p. 10

Sisson, Frederick - s/o George T. & Betsey M. Sisson, b Jul 12, 1877, d Jun 18, 1878, 11 mo

Sisson, George T. - George T. Sr & Betsey M. - b Jan 29, 1847, d Sep 18, 1880
Sissson, Harriet P. - d/o George T. Sr & Betsey M., b Jun 2, 1873, d May 2, 1889
Stannard, Emma T. Potter - d/o George Sr & Betsey R. Potter, b Oct 30, 1813, d Mar 2, 1852, m Ansel Stannard Sep 6, 1850
Stannard, Martha Hall - d Jun 9, 1847, 1st w/o Ansel Stannard
Stillman, George Chauncy - s/o William H. & Susan J., b 1865, d Mar 8, 1869
Stillman, Nina E. - d/o William H. & Susan J., b 1859, d Nov 30, 1860 Richburg, . NY, 3 yrs-10 mo
Tanner, Albert H. - b 1831, d Feb 28, 1859, m Alvina (or Alvira) G. Burdick Oct 20, 1846 at Clarksville NY
Tanner, Clarissa Brown - b Nov 4, 1801, d Dec 15, 1873, w/o John Tanner
Tanner, Elizabeth F. - d Nov 6, 1837
Tanner, John - b Sep 15, 1799, d Sep 6, 1870, m Clarissa Brown

p. 11

Wells, Daniel Babcock - s/o Joseph & Lydia Maxson, b Aug 15, 1811 Westerly RI, d Sep 12, 1871, m Mar 7, 1833 Sally Ann Burdick, m Dec 28, 1848 Harriet J. Lewis
Wells, Lucy Clarke - d/o Samuel & Lucy Maxson - b Apr 3, 1827 Andover NY, d Nov 18, 1916, w/o Samuel Wells
Wells, Emma - d/o Joseph & Lydia Maxson, b Jul 15, 1827, d Dec 1, 1878
Wells, Harriet J. Lewis - d/o Elijah Lewis, b Jan 10, 1822, d May 21, 1876
Wells, Joseph - Genesee Twsp., Allegany Co. NY pioneer, b Oct 14, 1785 RI, d Jun 1, 1837, m Lydia Maxson (1785-1861)
Wells, Joseph Willard - s/o Joseph & Lydia Maxson, b Feb 9, 1808 Westerly RI, d Sep 19, 1855
Wells, Lucy Clarke - d/o Samuel B. & Lucy Maxson Clarke, b 1818, d Dec 20, 1864, w/o Samuel Wells
Wells, Sally Ann Burdick - d/o Jabez & Mary A. Jaques, d Apr 29, 1846, w/o Daniel Babcock Wells
Wells, Samuel - s/o Joseph & Lydia Maxson, b Jul 27, 1817, d Nov 27, 1898, m Lucy Clarke, m Emily Clarke

p. 12

Wells, William Oscar - s/o Daniel B. & Sally A , d Oct 11, 1837
Willson, Augusta - d/o Hiram & Ann Ennis, d Feb 10, 1844, 2 yrs-28 da
Willson, Forest L. - s/o Hiram & Ann Ennis, d Feb 5, 1844, 4 yrs-11 mo -13 da
Worden, Green - d Dec 16, 1855, 63 yrs, m Louisa Eggleston
Worden, Louisa Eggleston - d Jan 19, 1871, 79 yrs, w/o Green Worden

Compiled in 1987 by Jerald S. DeGroff, Genesee Town Historian, Little Genesee, Allegany Co, NY
SDB Archives : B files -- Allegany County Cemetery Records.
IMS:1995

(ed note: The Little Rhode Island Cemetery records were included because they illustrate the early migration pattern of early Rhode Island families westward.)

IV. THE BUFFALO AREA CHURCHES

Clarence (Pembroke and Darien) SDB Church 1828-c1873
First organized at Greenman Settlement, near Alden, Clarence Twsp., Erie Co. NY
Some meetings held over line in Pembroke, Genesee Co.
Extended in Erie, Genesee, Niagara, Wyoming Co.'s: 199 members
In 1833 called Darien, in 1836 called Clarence until 1873
Mother church called North Branch as church began to subdivide

Record book 1

p. 5   Constituent Members

Luke Greenman
Jesse L. Greenman
Asa Greenman
Edward Saunders Jr
Thomas Williams Jr
John L. Burdick
Sybbel Greenman
Catherine Williams
Gideon Williams

Members

John W. Austin - ad 1830
Delila Harvey - ad 1830
Henry Clarke - ad 1831
Larenda Greenman - bp 1831
Olive Greenman - bp 1831
Mary Lyman - ad 1831
Genetia Greenman - ad 1831
George Butler - ad 1830
William Williams - ad 1830
Daniel Carpenter - ad 1830
Mary Carpenter - ad 1830
John Sheldon - ad 1830
Phebe Burdick - ad 1830
Lois Greenman - ad 1830
Luke Greenman - ad 1830
Cornelia Greenman - ad 1830
Hallet Greenman - ad 1830
Abagil Greenman - ad 1830
Nathan Greenman - ad 1830
Deborah Clark - ad 1831
Stephen Dye - ad 1832
Roswell Cottrell - ad 1832
Mary Cook - ad 1832
Harriet Greenman - ad 1832
Sarah Greenman - bp 1832
James Greenman - bp 1832

p. 6

Mary Greenman - ad 1833
Eld. N. V. Hull - ad 1833
Phalla Hull - ad 1833
Earl Potter - ad 1833
Joshua W. Burdick - ad 1833
Hannah Burdick - ad 1833
Catherine Butler - ad 1833
Thomas Richardson - ad 1833
William D. Cochran - ad 1833
Alice S. Green - ad 1833
Bariah G. Smith - ad 1833
Betsey Smith - ad 1833
Esther Fuller - ad 1834
Amos P. Richardson - ad 1834
Joel Jones - ad 1834
Catherine Jones - ad 1834
Farley F. Coon - ad 1834
Amy Coon - ad 1834
Eliza Richardson - ad 1834
Sophia Richardson - ad 1834
Nancy Harvey - 1834
Orran Jones - ad 1834
Margaret Saunders - ad 1834
Nancy Carpenter - ad 1834
Hannah Carpenter - ad 1834
Emeline Saunders - ad 1834
Lyman Pratt - ad 1834
Lucy Pratt - ad 1834
Pamela Saunders - ad 1836
Cyrena Saunders - ad 1836
Catherine Burdick - ad 1836
Lucy Hobridge - ad 1836
Sary Crandall - ad 1836
Mary Crandall - ad 1836
Hannah Crandall - ad 1836
Mary Burdick - ad 1836

In back of record book

Lois Greenman - dis 1832
J. W. Austin - rj 1832
Gideon Williams - rj 1832
Henry Clark - rj 1832
___?__ Clark rj 1832

Roswell Cottrell - rj 1834
Bercas G. Smith - rj 1834
Betsey Smith - rj 1835
Luke Greenman - rj 1835

CRR 19x.39 vault
First record book
Clarence NY SDB Church Records 1828-1842
also Darien-Cowlesville 1851-1855
IMS: 1995

Clarence SDB NY   1842-1861
Second record book (some duplication)

p. 2   Members 1842
Hamilton Hull
John F. Morgan and wife
Samuel Hunt
Abagail Hunt
John Cheesborough
John Moore
Emely Baker
Charles Rood
James Rood
Anna Mariah Greenman
Mary Greenman
Sister Below
Richard Day and wife - bp
Jesse Beman - bp
Mary E. Coon
p. 3
John Russell - bp
Hazard M. Ayres - bp
Cornelia Ayres
p. 4
William Silk - bp
Henry Cottrell - bp
Isaac Redner - bp
Albert Eldred - bp

Thomas Olcott - bp
David Thorngate - bp
John Hunt - bp
Caroline Olcott - bp
Mary Ann Finch - bp
Eliza Redner - bp
Peter Feller - bp
Luke Greenman - ad
Nelson Aylesworth - bp
Lucy Aylesworth - bp
Lyman Beman - bp
Mary Beman - bp
Lyman Burdick - bp
Sabrina Langworthy - bp
Malvina Dixson - bp
Eliza Noble - bp
Mary Ann McCaleb - bp
p. 5 1843
Francis Billiard - bp
Sabrina Billiard - bp
Henry Eldred - bp
Harrison Thomas - bp
Andrew Finch - bp
Sally Eldred - bp
Mary Jane Eldred - bp

Alvira Hunt - bp
Melissa Feller - bp
Harriet Post - bp
Hannah Carl - bp
Lemuel Potter - ad
Nancy Baldwin - bp
Susannah Jane Baldwin - bp
Melissa C. Baldwin - bp
Lewis G. Baldwin - bp
Levi Baldwin - bp
Werdin Wells - bp

p. 13 1844
Mary Hodgkess
Jacob Ward
C. Coburn
J. Fullmer

Peter Vandaventer
Lydia Fulmer
Sophronia Hatch
Frances Longmate
Enoch Longmate
Ann Longmate
Martha Vandarventer
Ira Hunt - bp

p. 25
Eld. A. L. Andrus - bp 1845,
    fr first day pastorate
Delorville Helton - bp 1846
Franklin Babcock - ad 1855
Eld. A. Lewis - ad 1860
Mary C. Lewis - ad 1860

CRR 19x.104   vault
Second record book
Clarence SDB Church 1842-61
IMS: 1995

Pendleton SDB Church 1846-1873
North of Clarence, Pentleton Twsp., Niagara Co.
First church set off from Clarence

Members 1846
p. 1
Eld. Lemon Andrus
Dea. Baily Curtis - dis Friendship 1854
William P. Longmate, clerk
Mrs. L. Andrus
Ann Longmate
___?___ Snow
___?___ Snow
John Fullmer
Lidda Fulmer
Martha Witt - rj 1848
___?___ Winters
Enoch Longmate - rj 1846
Frances Longmate - rj 1847
Mary Hodgkins - rj 1847
Aophrona Hatch - rj 1847
John Davis - fr Wilson
Content Davis - fr Wilson
Paulina Davis - fr Wilson
p. 5 1848-9
Limon B. Crandall
Limon Burdick
Rouse Burdick
Sarah Crandall - d 1850, 62 yrs

Hannah Mead - d 1850, 35 yrs
Mary Burdick - d 1851, 55 yrs
Phebe Burdick
Mary Bowen
Martha Burdick
Elvira A. Burdick
___?___ Winters
Harriet Davis - bp 1850
Paulina Davis
Delatreus Davis - bp 1850
Tereis Farnam - ad 1854
Sister Sherman - ad 1854
p. 15 1855 Members
William P. Longmate
John Fullmer
Rouse Burdick
Liman Burdick
Lymon B. Crandall
Ann Longmate - d 1862, 80 yrs
Lidda Fullmer
___?___ Andrus
Phebe Burdick
Mary Bowen
Martha Burdick
Elvira A. Burdick

CRR 19x.105   vault
The Pendleton SDB Record 1846-1870
IMS:1995

Darien Cowlesville SDB Church 1851-1873
Cowlesville in NW corner of Wyoming Co. NY,
Near Alden, Erie Co. NY
Second Church set off because Clarence area was so large

Petiton to be set off from Clarence 1851

Elisha Saunders
Robert Williams
John L. Burdick
John Sheldon
Jeremiah Barriett
Benjamin Clark
Stephen Stebbins
Stillman Burdick
Anson T. Saunders
Dennis Burdick
Almira Clark
Louisa Hoag
Sarah J. Saunders
Sophia Clark
Malinda Clark
Mary J. Williams
Martha Williams
Mary Saunders
Esther Davis
Lydia Hunt
Catherine Burdick

Eunice Robinson
Mary Hoag
Hannah Howard
Sophia Maxson
Cyrenia Saunders
Louisa Clark
Elizabeth Stebbins
Harriet Saunders
Mary Clark
Pamela Saunders
Calista Barrett
Hannah Austin
Arelia Blanchard
Olive Green
Hannah Saunders
Sarah Greenman
Samuel Hunt
Dea. Ethan Saunders
Nancy Saunders
Amy Harris

Darien - Cowlesville Record Book Membership List
Listed as South Branch of Clarence
and second church to be separated from Clarence
(Includes petitioners listed above).

p. 3 1851 Members
Elisha Saunders
George Davis
Robert Williams
Benjamin Clark
Dennis Burdick
Louisa Clark
Sophia Clark
Jeremiah Barrett
Stephen Stebbins
Anson P. Saunders
Sarah J. Saunders
Malinda Clarke

p. 4
Lydia Hunt
Caroline Burdick
Mary Hoag
Eliza Stebbins
Cyrenia Saunders
Louisa M. Hoag Hill
Welthy Clark Williams
Almira Clark
Calista Barrett
Hannah Saunders
Sarah Greenman
Esther Davis

Martha Williams
Catherine Burdick
Eunice Robinson
Hannah Howard
Sophia Maxson
Harriet Saunders
Mary Clark Taylor
Pamelia Saunders
Arelia Blanchard
Olive Greenman

Mary J. Williams
Ruth Stebbins - bp 1853
Arano Babcock - bp 1853
Ansel Brown - ad 1853
Caroline Saunders - bp 1853
Ruth Stebbins - bp 1853
Arano Babcock - bp 1853
Ansel Brown - bp
Caroline Saunders - bp 1853

CRR 19x.39 vault
Clarence NY Church Records 1828-1842
also Darien-Cowleville NY 1850-1855
IMS: 1995

Wilson SDB Church 1852-1862
Near Lake Ontario, E. Wilson, Wilson Twsp. Niagara Co. NY
Third church, Set off as branch of Pendleton Church,
sub-branch of Clarence

Members of Record
p. 10
Abreham Hill - clerk
Susan Hill
James Hill
Luke Sharman
Trudah Symons
Delotreus Davis - chosen deacon

CRR 19x.105 vault
Pendleton SDB Church Record 1846-1870
IMS: 1995

Clarence and Pendleton SDB Church 1875-1883
Rapids, Erie Co. NY
Fourth church: remnants of Clarence, Darien, Cowlesville, and Pendleton
Last members joined First Alfred

Members 1875
John Fullmer
Lydia Fullmer
William P. Longmate
Hannah Commins
Samuel Hunt
John F. Morgan
Lyman B. Burdick
Jesse H. Beeman
Mary Burdick
Fanny Longmate
Sybil F. Burdick
Alvina A. Burdick
Mary C. Bowen

p. 2
Robert Kenny - bp 1878
Hannah Kenny - bp 1878
Phebe Bowin - bp 1878
Eld. Charles A. Burdick - ad 1879
Amanda Burdick w/o Charles - ad 1879
Adele Burdick d/o Charles - ad 1879
Sarah A. Burdick Gillings - bp 1878
Lucy Burdick - ad 1880
Amos T. Bowen - ad 1880
Rouse K. Burdick - ad 1880
Esther Beeman - bp 1880
Fanny Downey - bp 1880
Dea. William P. Longmate - d
Hannah Commins - d
Mary Burdick - d
Jesse H. Beeman - d
Lyman B. Burdick - d
Dea. John F. Morgan - b VT 1812, d Nov 14, 1896
Mrs. John F. Morgan - d Nov 27, 1890

CRR 19x.104   vault
Clarence SDB Record Book 1842-61
IMS:1995

Persia Seventh Day Baptist Church
1832-1858

Persia, Perrysburg Twsp., NW Cattaraugus Co. NY

Constituent Members

p.1

Hosea Whitford - ad 1832 fr First Brookfield, d Nov 17, 1843
Elizabeth Whitford - ad 1832 fr First Brookfield
Stephen Whitford - ad 1832 fr First Brookfield
Cornelia Whitford d/o Elnathan Maxson - ad 1832 fr First Brookfield, d Apr 3, 1845
Hosea Brown - ad 1832 fr First Brookfield, rj
Hannah Brown - ad 1832 fr First Brookfield, rj
Silas Burdick - ad 1832 fr Third Brookfield, rj Jan 2, 1842
Emma Babcock - ad 1832 fr Second Brookfield

Members

Oliver C. Babcock - bp 1832
Delos C. Burdick - bp 1832
Amy Babcock - bp 1832, d Feb 1838
Matilda Thorngate - ad 1832, dis
George Thorngate - bp 1832
Welcome A. Gardner - bp 1832, d Dec 1837
Elizabeth Burdick - bp 1832, d Aug 31, 1841
Alphanso G. Burdick - bp 1832, rj 1843
Alvah Brown - bp 1832, d
John Babcock - ad 1833 fr First Brookfield
Demaris Babcock - ad 1833 fr First Brookfield
Ann Crandall - ad 1833 fr Third Brookfield
Elbridg Eddy - ad 1834 fr Middlebury
Eunice Eddy - ad 1834 fr Middlebury
Allen Prentice - bp 1834, went to WI 1845
Eliza Prentice - bp 1834, went to WI 1845
George C. Babcock - bp 1834
Almira Babcock - bp 1834
Herman A. Hull - bp 1834, dis
William A. Babcock - bp 1834, dis
Leroy Burdick - bp bp 1834
Ira B. Brown - bp 1834, rj
Asher Brown - bp 1834, rj
Hannah Burdick - ad 1834
William Crandall - bp 1836, rj 1844
Benjamin F. Babcock - bp 1836
Paul B. Crandall - bp 1836, rj
Nancy Crandall - bp 1836, rj
Sarah Brown - bp 1836, rj

p. 2

Harry Blakely - bp 1837, d Aug 1837
Catherine Loomer - bp 1837, dis 1843
Delormey Loomer - bp 1837, dis 1843
Sebrina Greenman - bp 1837
Russell Burdick - ad fr Methodist Church 1837, dis
Sally Hawkins - ad 1837
Fanny Blakely - ad fr Forestville, d Apr 10, 1844
Mary Ackley - bp 1837
Loiza Wattenpaugh - bp 1837, rj 1843
Abigail Bassett - bp 1837, rj 1840
Sally Stewert - ad 1837, dis
Marie Kellogg - bp 1837
Huldy Randall - bp 1837
Sarrah Randall - bp 1837, rj
Lorry Randall - bp 1837
Phebe Crandall - bp 1837
Welthy Blakely - bp 1837
Uriah Hawkins - bp 1837, rj 1847
Lewis Pierce - bp 1837
Eliza Pierce - bp 1837
Elery Crandall - bp 1837, rj 1843
William Crandall - bp 1837, rj
Benjamin Peters - bp 1837, rj 1843
Adeline Burdick - bp 1837, dis
Nowel Hockins - bp 1837
Adolphin Burdick - bp 1837, dis
Hugh Campbell - bp 1838, rj 1841
Emma Campbell - bp 1838

p. 3

Lewis Crandall - bp 1839, rj 1842
Elisha Randall - bp 1839
Stephen Hockins - bp 1839, rj 1847
Alexander Hockins - bp 1839
Henry Brown - bp 1839
Franklin Brown - bp 1839, rj
Marcus Brown - bp 1839, rj
Betsey Ackler - bp 1839
Lucy Randall - bp 1839

Phebe Whitford - bp 1839
Kezia Peters - bp 1839, rj
Vernan Hull - ad 1839, dis
Ruhannah Serbner - bp 1839
Philena Wattenpaugh - bp 1839
Fidelia Pease - bp 1839
Mary Rhedfield - bp 1839
Lovena Walbridg - bp 1839, rj 1843
John Brown - ad 1839 fr First Brookfield
Fidelia Brown - ad 1839 fr First Brookfield, dis 1842
Mrs. Malida Hull - ad 1839 fr Clarence, dis
Ruth Goodwin - bp 1839
Marck T. Goodwin - bp 1839
Sally Sanden - bp 1839
Nathan Beverly - bp 1839
William H. Rhedfield - ad 1839 fr First Day Baptist, dis
Abigail Saunders - bp 1839
Charles Saunders - bp 1839
Gensha Saunders - ad 1839 fr Second Brookfield
Manlius Marsh Bush - bp 1839
Eliza Bush - bp 1839
Sarah Camp - bp 1839
Mary Smith - bp 1839, d Apr 22, 1842
Justus Blakely - ad 1839 fr First Alfred
Eleanor Atkins - ad 1839

p. 4
Hazad M. Ayres - ad 1841, dis 1842
Cornelia Ayres - ad 1841, dis
Abel Saunders - bp 1843
Eld. Thomas E. Babcock - ad 1843, dis
Hannah M. Babcock - ad 1843
Hiram Blakely - bp 1843
Henry Thorngate - bp 1843, dis
Charles Thorngate - bp 1843, dis
Mary Ann Thorngate - bp 1843, dis
Hannah Thorngate - bp 1843, dis
Francis M. Babcock - bp 1843
Henry Babcock - bp 1843
Noel Hawkins Jr - bp 1843
Fidealia Eddy - bp 1843

Carlos C. Eddy - bp 1843
John Babcock - ad 1843
Sarah A. Whitford - ad 1843
Damarias Babcock 2nd - bp 1843, dis
Hannah Prentice - bp 1843, dis
Silas Burdick - ad 1843, rest 1844
Jane Babcock - bp 1844
George Brown - bp 1844
Charles P. Rood - ad 1845, dis
Manna Hitchock - ad 1845, rj
Angeline Burdick - ad 1845, d
Nathan Randall Jr - ad 1845
Julia H. Randall - ad 1845
Eld. Ray Green - ad 1847, dis
Jane Green - ad 1847
Miss Ursula Green - bp Jul 1837, dis
Chauncey Satterlee - bp 1847

p. 10
Lebbius M. Cottrell - ad 1852
Lucy Maria Cottrell - ad 1852
Betsey Burdick - ad 1854
John Crandall - bp 1852
Lisa Crandall - bp 1852
Polly Vincent - bp 1852
Polly Saunders - bp 1853
Mary Hawkins - bp 1854
Hiram Vincent - bp 1854
Jeremy Green - ad 1854
Lucy Green - ad 1854

p. 11
Van Ranslear Green - ad 1854
Alexander Hawkins - ad 1854
Albert N. Babcock - bp 1854
Otsy O. Blakely - bp 1854
Rosalthe Randall - bp 1854
Emeline Hawkins - bp 1854
Mary Green - bp 1854
Adeline Eddy - bp 1854
Louisa Hammond - bp 1854
Achsa Babcock - bp 1854
Julia Babcock - bp 1854
Lydia Camp - bp 1854

CRR 19x.100   vault
Persia SDB Church Records 1832-1854
IMS:1995

V. NORTHWESTERN PENNSYLVANIA SEVENTH DAY BAPTIST CHURCHES

First Hebron SDB Church (Crandall Hill)
1833-
Hebron Twsp., Potter Co., PA
RD#2 Coudersport PA

Constituent Members
as listed in the Centenial Celebration Book 1833-1933
Organized February 10, 1833

George Stillman
Jesse M. Greenman
Ezekiel Main
Nathan Main
Elias Wells
Stephen Coon
David N. Stillman
Sylvia Coon
Sally Main

Betsy Greenman
Fanny Reynolds
Bridget Stillman
Angenet Coon
Betsy Hull
Roxy Hull
Evania Wells
Sally Coon

List from the Earliest Extant Record Book

1833
George Stillman
Jesse M. Greenman
Sylvia Coon - dis
Elisha Coon - dis '43
Lorenzo Coon - dis '43
Stephen H. Hydorn
Miranda Stillman - dis
Juliann Reynolds - dis
Ozias Sparks - dis
Alanson Stillman - dis
Sally Wells - d Apr 17 '53
James Greenman
Sardinia Wells
Stephen W. Coon, dis

1842
George W. Stillman
A.R. Stillman
Joseph Stillman
Simeon Luce
Stephen P. Reynolds
Electra Greenman - d Jan 23 '59

Sylvia Coon
Esther Coon - dis '50
Eleanor Hydorn
Juliann Coon - dis
Huldah Heges
Delia (pos Hydorn) - bp

1843
Almeron P. Stillman - dis '44
Sylvestor Greenman - dis '44

1844
Henry T. Reynolds - dis
I. Algernon Brock - dis
Isaac Brock
Sally Stillman
Deadamia Greenman - dis
Esther Wells - d Jan 1 '90
Hannah Stillman - d Jun 25 '83
Lavinia Stillman - dis
Rowse Babcock

1845
Sally Thibbe

1843
Carolyn Stillman

People dismissed 1845 to form Ulysses SDB Church Potter Co PA

Thomas Hallock
Ruth Gibbs - bp
Nancy Thibbe - bp
Noah Halleck - bp
Emma Harris - bp
David Gibbs - bp
Herman Palmer
Sally Thibbe

Martin L. Dean
Eli Thibbe - bp
James Thibbe - bp
Sally Ann Halleck - bp
Martha P. Dean - bp
Samuel Gibbs Jr - bp
Hulda Palmer Slade

Hebron Membership Continued

1844
Mary Stillman
Sarah Brock
Amy Brock
Lucinda Babcock - dis
Mary Ann Greenman
Orpha Stillman
Almina Brock
E. C. Hydorn
Sally Ann Wells

1845
Caroline Halley - bp
James Lewis - d '65

1846
Wealthy Spark
Elizabeth Sparks
Jane Hydorn - bp
William Greenman - bp
___?___ Sutherland
George McCoon - bp, dis
Lorenzo N. Babcock - dis
Franklin Babcock - dis
William C. Reynolds - bp

1847
Albert White
Fanny Greenman - ad Oct '44
Silas Shay
Sally Shay

1844
Sarah Reynolds - bp
Therissa Main - bp
Louise Hydorn - bp
Mary Brock - bp
Andrew Brock - bp
J. P. Randall - ad fr 1st Day Baptist,
    dis Mar 15 '59

1850
Henry Dingman - bp
Albert Reed - bp, dis Jun 20 '59
Joel Randall - bp, dis Jun 20 '59
Electra Lynch - bp

1851
Joseph Randall - bp
Maryjane Reynolds - bp

1859
Hiram W. Babcock - bp
Matilda C. Babcock

1853
Lewis Hall - bp
Romanze Luce - bp
Nancy J. White

1856
Sarah A. Randall - bp
Celeste Reynolds - bp
Mary L. Stillman - bp
Lavinia Brock - bp
Persis Davis - dis '69
Joel P. Randall Jr - rst

1858
Rosewell Burton - bp
Diana Burton - bp
Lucy Ferron - bp
Silas S. Greenman - bp
Sulivan Hydorn - bp, d Jan 18 '62
S. Elvira Stillman - bp
Orlando Feron - (already bp)

1859
Andred Ferron - bp
Orvilla Luce - bp
William Dingman - bp
Albert Reed - rst

1860
Elizabeth Hall
Jane Green

1862
Joel P. Randall - rst
Maria Stillman - bp
A. H. Ostrander - bp
Louisa Reed - bp
Elizabeth Burdick - bp
Ann Mowatt - bp, dis 1869
Henrietta Berkhardt - bp
Mary E. Green
Leroy R. Burdick
Esther Burdick
Elnora M. Green - bp
1865
Rosannah Brock - bp

1866
S. R. Wheeler
Sophia Wheeler
Caroline Hawley
Sarah Ayres - bp
1867
Lillian Reed - bp
Polly A. Luce - bp
A. H. Halleck
Samuel Gibbs - rec fr Ulysses
Susannah Gibbs - rec fr Ulysses
Ruth Gibbs - rec fr Ulysses
Linus Evans - rec fr Ulysses
June Harris - rec fr Ulysses
Hannah Hallack - rec fr Ulysses

Transcribed from the first record book of Hebron PA SDB Church 1833-1862 in posession of church clerk

SECOND RECORD BOOK OF HEBRON PA
Names of Members June 30, 1867

p. 20-21
George Stillman - constituent member, d Aug 16 '67 76 yrs 5 mo
J. M. Greenman - constituent member, dis
Elizabeth Greenman - constituent member, dis, d Mar 5'71 73 yrs 8 mo
Fanny Reynolds - constituent member, d May 14 '91
William H. Hydorn - ad 1836; d Dec 4 '97 or'98
Elenor Hydorn - ad 1836, d Aug 11 '86
Alanson Stillman - ad 1836, d Apr 28 '92
J. A. R. Greenman - ad 1836, dis
George W. Stillman - bp Jul 16 '42, d Aug 1 '78(?)
A. R. Stillman - ad Jul 16 '42, dis
Joseph Stillman - ad Jul 16 '42, dis
Sylvester Greenman - ad Mar 2'44, dis
p. 22-23
Almond Brock - ad Mar 2 '44, dis
Isaac Brock - ad 1844, d Ap r'79
Amy Brock - ad 1844, d Feb 7, 1904
Sarah Stillman - w/o C. Stearns, ad 1843; d Sep 11 '88
Caroline Stillman - ad 1843, dis
Orpha Stillman - w/o William C. Reynolds, ad 1844; d '78 (?)
Mary Ann Greenman - w/o G. W. Stillman, ad Mar 2 '44
Almina Brock - w/o Henry Dingman, ad Mar 2 '44, d Jan 24, 1920
Sarah Brock - w/o Simeon Lance & E. D. Ayars, ad Mar 2 '44, d Apr 13 '98
Cordelia Hydorn - w/o E. C., bp Mar 2 '44; d Mar 22 '71
William R. Greenman - bp Jan 3 '46, dis
William C. Reynolds - bp Jun 3 '46, d Jul 7, 1904
Fanny Greenman - ad '48, dis

p. 24-25
Louisa Hydorn - w/o Slyvester Greenman, bp Oct 21 '48, dis
Mary Brock - w/o William Dingman, bp Oct 21 '48, d Dec 18, 1917
J. A. Brock - bp Oct 21 '48, d Nov 20, 1902
Henry Dingman - bp Dec 14 '50, d Aug 19 '97
L. H. Hall - bp Mar 26 '53, dis Aug 30 '90
Romanzo Luce - bp Mar 26 '53, dis
Sarah A. Randall - bp Oct 11 '56, d Jan 25, 1928
Celestia Reynolds - w/o Elno E. Burdick & Culver, bp Oct 11 '56 d Jun 2 '81
Mary L. Stillman - w/o Henry A. Ostrander, bp Oct 11 '56, d Jun 2 '81
Lavina Brock - w/o George Kenyon, bp Oct 11 '56, dis
J. P. Randall Jr - rec back '56, d Nov 14, 1927
Diana Burton - bp Nov 27 '58, dis Mar 1'74
Lucy Ferran - Broadman, St. Croix Co. WI, bp Mar 27 '58, dis May 2 '72

p. 26-27
S. S. Greenman - bp Nov 27 '58, dis Nov 25 '71
S. Elvira Stillman - w/o H. E. Babcock, bp Nov 27 '58, d Feb 7 '73
Orlando Ferrand - Boardman, St. Croix Co., PA, ad '58, dis May 24 '72
Andrew Ferrand - bp Feb 13 '59, dis
Orvilla Luce - Broadman, St. Croix Co. WI, bp Feb 13 '59, dis May 24 '72
William Dingman - bp Feb 13 '59, d Aug 4 '94
Albert Reed - rec back Feb 13 '59, d
Jane Green - ad 1860, d May 1, 1900
Elizabeth Hall - ad Dec 9 '60, dis Aug 30 '90
J. P. Randall - rec back Feb 22 '62, d Jun 19, 1903
Mariah Stillman - w/o N. Wardner fr Roulette PA, bp May 10 '62 d Sep 8 '93
A. H. Ostrander - bp May 10 '62, dis Jan 16'87
Louisa Reed - bp May 10 '62, dis

p. 28-29
Elizabeth Burdick - bp May 1 '62, d May 6 '72
Elnora M. Green - w/o Jacob Snyder, bp May 10 '62, dis '70
Leroy Burdick - ad Dec 20 '62, d Jul 22, 1905
Esther Burdick - ad Dec 20 '62, d Feb 23, 1905
Rosannah Brock - bp Oct 21 '65, dis July 5, 1902
S. R. Wheeler - ad Jul 21 '66, dis
Sophia Wheeler - ad Jul 21 '66, dis
Caroline Hawley - w/o S. Chamberlin & William S. Burdick
    ad Sep 22 '66, d Apr 12, 1911
Sarah Ayres - w/o R. H. Emerson, bp Nov 24 '66, d May 22, 1919
Lillian Reed - w/o ___?___ Watson, bp Jan 5 '67, dis Jan 16'94
Polly A. Luce - w/o Isaac Baker Jr, bp Jan 5 '67, d Oct 24, 1916
N. H. Halleck - ad fr Ulysses Church '61, d Nov 18 '94
Samuel Gibbs Jr - ad fr Ulysses Church July '61, d Dec 31 '88 70 yrs

p. 30-31
L. Evans - ad July 15 '61 fr Ulysses Church, dis
Hannah Halleck - ad Jul '61, fr Ulysses Church, d
Melissa Halleck Perkins - ad Jul 15 '61 fr Ulysses Church, dis 1921
Simeon Luce - ad Jul '42, d Sep 1 '87
Susannah Gibbs - ad Jul '61 fr Ulysses Church
Ruth Gibbs - ad Jul '61 fr Ulysses Church, d Jun 27 '88
Jane Johnson - ad Ju '61 fr Ulysses Church, d
Joanna Matteson - w/o Richard Mitchell, bp Jul 27 '67, d 1925

S. Jennie Lovell - w/o J. Edward Porter, bp Jul 27 '67, dis May 24 '72
Angeline Green - w/o A. A. Reed, bp Jul 27 '67, dis Aug 8 '91
Lydia Brock - ad Jul 2 '67, d Oct 2 '68
Alma Gibbs - w/o Egbert Ostrander, ad Nov 23 '67, dis Jan '94
Egbert Ostrander - bp Nov 23 '67, dis '70
Elno E. Burdick - ad Nov '67, d Aug 16 '80

p. 32-33
Samuel Gibbs - ad Jul '61 fr Ulysses Church, d Sep 18 '67 76 yrs 11 mo 24 da
Sardinia Wells - w/o Bruce Pierce & C. Stearns, ad '36 d 1913
Mary Stillman - w/o L. French, ad '44, dis
Roswald Emerson - ad '69, d Jun 19, 1924
Perry Brock - bp Nov 13 '69, d Feb 12, 1929
Harriet Emerson - w/o F. A. Ayars, bp Jan 30 '70
Ada Stillman - w/o Jefferson Matteson, ad Jan 30 '70 d Jul 15 '84
Ida Williams - bracketed in with Ada Stillman
Freeman Ayars - bp Jan 30 '70
Isaac H. Dingman - bp Mar 19 '70, d Apr 26, 1922
Sarah Brock - bp Mar 19 '70, d Feb 12, 1921
Jane Atkins - ad '70, d Jan 24 '97
Eld. Herbert E. Babcock - ad Dec. 10 '70, dis
John Dingman Sr - bp '71, d Aug 6 '78

p. 34-35
Elijah L. Ayres - bp '71, d May 27, 1905
George P. Kenyon - bp '71, dis
Jefferson Matteson - bp '71, dis Sep 17 '82
Walter Green - bp Jan 14 '71, d Mar 1, 1923
Webster Green - bp Jan 14 '71, dis Jul 15 '93
Leroy Burdick Jr - bp Jan 14 '71, d Oct 19 '74
Elwin G. Burdick - bp Jan 14 '71, d Sep 6, 1935
Mary M. Burdick - Jan 14 '71, dis Feb 22 '79, d Mar 30, 1909
Nancy Ayres - bp Jan 14 '71, d Jun 2 '87
Adelbert L. Luce - bp Jan 14 '71, dis May 21 '82
Roxana Emerson - ad Mar 4 '72, d Feb 17 '91
Loretta May Stillman - w/o __?__ Cone, bp Nov 29 '73, d Apr 18 '83
Lottie Ayars - w/o __?__ Millard, bp Nov 29 '73, d Nov 16 '84
Jennie Randall - w/o W. W. Thompson, bp Aug 1 '73, d Aug 28, 1946
Flora Gibbs - w/o __?__ Loup, bp Aug 1 '74, d

p. 36-37
Moses Atkinson - bp Aug 1 '74, d Dec 27, 1910
Isaac Baker Jr - bp Aug 1 '74, joined 1st Day Baptist Church
Eve Dingman - bp May 29 '75, d Jan 9, 1918
Laura Dingman - w/o __?__ Gridley, bp May 29 '75, dis Mar 29 '98
      to join First Alfred
Adelbert D. Millard - bp Sep 18 '75, dis
Eliza R. Millard - w/o C. Witter, bp Apr 1 '76, dis Oct 2 '81
Melvin M. Millard - bp Apr 1 '76, dis
Lincoln E. Burdick - bp Apr 1 '76, d Aug 2, 1934
William L. Burdick - bp Apr 1 '76, dis Sep '82, d Feb 29, 1952
Minnie H. Burdick - w/o John Miller, bp Sep '76, d
Ella M. Burdick - w/o Roscoe Stearns, bp Sep '76, d Oct 14, 1941

Clara J. Emerson - w/o __?__ Strait, bp Sep '76, Jan 1918
Clara R. Brock - w/o __?__ Card, bp Sep '76
Alice L. Swartout - w/o __?__ George, bp Se p'76, d Nov 12, 1909
Mary A. Nichols - w/o __?__ Tracy, dis to 1st Day Baptist Church '98, d 1917
Alice L. Swartout w/o ___?___ George, burned to death in her house 1909
Nettie Luce - __?__ Baker, bp Sep '76, dis
Alfred R. Reed - bp Sep '76, dis Jul 16 '93
Charles Reynolds - bp Sep '76, d Feb 4, 1925
John R. Millard - bp May 6 '86, dis Sep 15 '93
Fanny Millard - bp May 6 '76, d May 23 '77

p. 38-39
Charles Ostrander - bp 1876, dis 1893
Anner Randall - bp 1876, d Feb 21, 1917
Mrs. Charlotte E. Groves - ad 1879, dis 1893
Charles Greenman - bp 1880, dis 1891
Mrs. Elizabeth Place - ad 1880 fr and Alfred, d Apr 8, 1886
Mrs. Charlotte Lamberton - ad 1880 fr Bell's Run, d Mar 3, 1887
Ada M. Lambeton (Wakely) - ad 1880, dis 1895
Fanny P. Burdick - bp 1880, d winter of 1844
Archy V. Tracy - bp 1880, dis 1898 to 1st Day Baptist at Coudersport
Charles A. Lamberton - bp 1881, dis 1893
Mrs. Mary Reed - bp 1882, dis
Edith Randall w/o George Bickford, bp 1882, d Dec 2, 1916
Mrs. Mary Randall - bp 1882, d 1949
John Baker - bp 1882, dis

p. 40-41
Eld. George P. Kenyon ,- ad 1883, dis
Mary M. Kenyon - ad 1883, d Mar 30, 1949
Alice Perkins - bp 1884, dis
Anna Ball - bp 1884, dis 1900
Frank Ball - bp 1884, dis 1900
Joseph Baker - bp 1886, dis 1921
Franklin P. Atkinson - bp 1886, d Oct 1, 1944
Lydia Brock Baker - bp 1886, dis
Mettie Dolley Burdick Reynolds - bp 1886, dis
Alice Baker - bp 1886, d Feb 13, 1906
Flora L. G. Burdick - ad 1889, dis 1892
Mrs. Elwin G. Burdick - bp 1890, d Apr 28, 1928
Mrs. Philip Matteson - bp 1890
Miss Jennie Brock - bp 1890, dis 1926
Alice Emerson Dingman - Dingman - bp 1890, d Jul 23, 1951
Belle Randall Snyder - bp 1890, d Aug 21, 1951
George Dingman - bp 1890, d May 29, 1942
Willis Brock - bp 1890, d 1944

p. 42-43
Mrs. S. P. Reynolds - ad 1890, d Dec 17, 1918
Chester A. Burdick - bp 1890, d Mar 15, 1923
Almond D. Dingman - bp 1890, d Sep 26, 1924
Grove Mitchell - bp 1891
Martha J. Atkinson Combs - bp 1891, d Jun 17, 1942

Cora Crandall Burdick - bp 1891, d 1949
John C. Burdick - ad 1891, d Jan 28, 1899
Mrs. John C. Burdick - ad 1891, d
S. P. Reynolds - ad 1891, d May 2, 1902
G. L. Burdick - bp 1891, dis
William Matteson - bp 1891, dis Munsey PA
Mrs. William Matteson - bp 1891, d Mar 27, 1899
Miss Gennie Reynolds - bp 1891, d Mar 12, 1918
Frank O. Knickerbocker - bp 1895, dis
Rev. A. Lawrence - ad 1895, dis 1896
Emma Atkinson Lamb - bp 1895
George M. Barber - ad 1899 fr Alfred, d Jan 5, 1910
Mrs. George M. Barber - ad 1899 fr Alfred , dis 1909
Dennis Carpenter - ad 1899 fr S.D. Adventists, d Dec 18, 1920
Mrs. Dennis Carpenter - ad 1899 fr S. D. Adventists, dis

p. 44-45
Miss Maude Barber - bp 1899, dis 1903
M. E. Collins- bp 1899, d Dec 3, 1904
Mrs. M. E. Collins - bp 1899, dis 1921
Miss Lillian Dingman w/o A. W. Thompson - bp 1899
Miss Rena Randall w/o Ray Culbertson - bp 1899, dis 1927 to United Brethern
Mrs. Susie Matteson - bp 1899, dis 1914, d Apr 1937

Transcribed from second record book of Hebron PA SDB Church
1867-1954
in possession of church clerk
IMS:1994

Ulysses SDB Church 1845-c1910

Ulysses, Ulysses Twsp., Potter Co. PA
At one time called Lewisville
Eighteen miles fr First Hebron

Members dismissed from First Hebron in 1845

Martin L. Dean
Thomas Hallock
Ruth Gibbs
Nancy Thibbe
Noah Hallock
Emma Harris
David Gibbs

Herman Palmer
Eli Thibbe
James Thibbe
Sally Ann Halleck
Martha P. Dean
Hannah Hallock
Sally Thibbe

Other Members

Samuel Gibbes Jr

Huldah Palmer Slade

Members rejoining First Hebron in 1867

Samuel Gibbs Jr
Susannah Gibbs
Ruth Gibbs
Linus Evans

June Harris
Hannah Hallack
Jane Johnson

From a letter in 1902 by Sarah A. H. Lindsey of Wellesville B-file
First Hebron SDB Record Book in possession of church clerk
Seventh Day Baptists in Europe and America. Vol II, p. 742
Seventh Day Baptist General Conference 1910

Allegheny River SDB Church

(Port Allegheny, Roulette) 1871-c1877
Liberty, Liberty Twsp., McKean Co., PA

J. L. Huffman - Association Evangelist
Members of Record-
Leroy Lyman
Thankful Lyman - d 1890
Sybil Lyman w/o Orlando Burdick
Celesta E. Lyman w/o John L. Smith
Bell J. Lyman w/o J. A. Sampson

Seventh Day Baptists in Europe and America. Vol II, p. 745
Seventh Day Baptist General Conference 1910
Marriages and deaths fr The Sabbath Recorder files

Hebron Center Seventh Day Baptist Church
1871-1953

also called Greenman Settlement, 4 miles east of First Hebron
RFD Coudersport, Potter Co. PA

Constituent Members

p. 496

J. M. Greenman - ad 1871, d Dec 18, 1878
Elizabeth Greenman - ad 1871, d Mar 5, 1871
J. A. R. Greenman - ad 1871, d
Fanny M. Greenman - ad 1871, d Aug 7, 1893
B. F. Greenman - bp 1871, rj 1881
Sylvester Greenman - ad 1871, d Nov 7, 1895
Louisa H. Greenman - ad 1871, dis
William R. Greenman - ad 1871, d Nov 2, 1888
Joseph Clair Jr - bp 1871, d
Silas P. Hemphill - ad 1871, d
Harley Knickerbocker - ad 1871, d
Frederic K. Welch - ad 1871
Elizabeth Welch - ad 1871, d Aug 22, 1877
Phineas Goodwin - bp 1871, rj 1872
Adelia Goodwin - bp 1871, rj 1872
Emily Booth - bp 1871, rj 1881
Mary J. Clair w/o William - bp 1871, d Sep 17, 1902

Other Members of Record

Hugh Booth - ad 1871, rj 1881, d
Adelia Ball - bp 1874, d
Emaline Ball White - bp 1874, dis
Solomon Chamberlin - ad 1874, d Jul 28, 1893
Mary M. Clair - bp 1874, d
Rosaltha Clair Mattison - bp 1874
Euphemia (Holly) Hemphill - bp 1874
M. Jane Clair w/o Edward - bp 1874
Ida Clair Roseboom - bp 1874
Alsie Ball Sherwood - bp 1874, d Apr 17, 1894
Electa E. Sherman Nelson - bp 1874
Rosa White - bp 1874
Charles White - bp 1874
Ambrose Ball - ad 1874, d Apr 10, 1904
C. D. McKee - ad 1874, dis 1894
Electa White - ad 1874, d Apr 1876
Mary Dibble - ad 1874, d
S. W. Dibble - ad 1874, d
Harriet Sherwood - bp 1876, d Mar 1893

p. 498

Flora Greenman - bp 1876, dis 1889
Mrs. Harris - bp 1876, d
Orlando Greenman - bp 1876, d Jan 25, 1896
Joseph Clair Sr - ad 1880, d
Maria Clair - ad 1880
Emma Shaw - ad 1880
Frederick Emerson - bp 1880
Marcus E. Clair - bp 1880
James Ball - bp 1880, d Jun 12, 1931
Julia Shaw Winson - bp 1880, d
Ella M. Hemphill Crocker - bp 1880, rj 1904
Luman E. Clair - bp 1880
Flora DeEtte McKee - bp 1880, dis 1888
Lovina Hemphill - bp 1880, dis 1896
Walter Hemphill - bp 1880
Hattie Clair - bp 1880
Nellie Clair Swift - bp 1880, rj 1904
Ephraim Emerson - ad 1880, d Jul 10, 1894
Lewis Ball - bp 1891, d Dec 8, 1935
Louella Ball - bp 1891, d
Alta Clair Stillman - bp 1891
Dillar Lewis - ad 1891, d Jan 7, 1892
Rosie Clair Redner - bp 1891, d Jan 17, 1935
Evilena Clair Gale - bp 1891, d Jan 10, 1910
Bertha White Bly - bp 1891, dis
Electa Ball - ad 1891, d Apr 20, 1898
Vina Kenyon - ad 1891, d Jul 5, 1923
Mortemor Kenyon - ad 1891, d Jun 1932
Edward Clair - ad 1891, d Jan 1916
Andrea Lewis - ad 1891, d
Charles Sherwood - ad 1891, d Jan 27, 1925
Fredrick Degrater - ad 1891
May Hemphill - bp 1896, d Jun 26, 1900
Miss H. C. Monson - ad 1896, d
John Clair Sr - bp 1896, d Feb 1920

CRR 1992.26 vault
Hebron Center SDB Church Records 1871-1940
IMS:1995

Shinglehouse SDB Church 1883-1920
Shinglehouse, Potter Co. PA
Forty members widely scattered

Members

p. 15
Asa Burdick - Sep 25, 1870
Mary Burdick - Sep 25, 1870
Harrison B. Smith - Mar 2, 1878
Willard C. Palmer - Mar 2, 1878
Alsina Palmer - Mar 2, 1878
George Trask - Nov 23, 1878
Horace Howe - Jun 26, 1880
Mrs. J. H. Howe - Nov 15, 1879
Emma L. Cartwright - Sep 25, 1870
Mrs. L. S. Casteline - Nov 11, 1870
Dea. B. O. Burdick - Sep 25, 1870
Mrs. Mary Burdick - Sep 25, 1870
Emmet Burdick - Sep 25, 1870
Mrs. Ida Burdick - Sep 25, 1870
Mrs. Joseph Marsh - May 1, 1883

p. 16
B. O. Burdick & wife - dis Mar 4, 1888 to KS

p. 17   Jan 1881
Mrs. Catherine Warner -
H. S. Burdick
Mrs. Melissa Bridge
Nimrod Lanphere
Edgar Wells
Orson Maxson
Harriet Wilbur
Libbie Mix
Ester Wells
Rhoda Maxson
Ester Wells
Dea. Clark S. Wells

Alton Maxson
Dea. Charles B. Wilbur
Hattie Wells
Sallie Lanphere - d
Harriet Woren
T. W. F. Sage
Abigal Sage
Alfonso North - dp Jun 12, 1887
Bell North - d
Mary Mawfet Clemons

p. 18
Mary Bridge - d
Samuel & Mary How dis 1890
Mary Viola Trask - Jan 12, 1889

p. 19
J. J. Kenyon - May 1, 1883
Mrs. J. J. Kenyon - May 1, 1883
Mrs. Mary Lanphere - May 1, 1883
Mrs. Andrew Bradford
Mrs. Melissa Bridge - Aug 1884
Miss Ida Davis - bp Jun 6, 1885
Miss May Bridge - bp May 1, 1886
Miss Grace Robison - bp May 1, 1886
Miss Ella Morris - bp May 29, 1886
Samuel Howe - ad Jul 10, 1886
Mary Howe - ad Jul 10, 1886
Charles R. Voorhees - ad Jul 24, 1886
Mary A. Voorhees - ad Jul 24, 1886
Mary Viola Trask - ad Jan 1, 1887
Eld. George P. Kenyon - ad Jan 1, 1887
Mary M. Kenyon - Jan 1, 1887
Lydia J. Benehoff - Sep 12, 1891

List of Resident Members June 1891

p. 20
Mrs. Catherine Warner
Edgar Wells
Harriet Willber
Ester Wells
Hattie Wells
Clark Wells - d
Charles B. Wilber - d
J. J. Kenyon
Mrs. J. J. Kenyon

Mrs. Andrew Bradford
Mrs. George Morehouse
Ella Morris
C. R. Voorhees
Mary A. Voorhees
G. P Kenyon
Mary M. Kenyon
George Trask
W. C. Palmer
Mrs. W. C. Palmer

H. S. Burdick
Stella Voorhees
p. 21
Ase Burdick - nr, d
Mary Burdick - nr
P. C. Cartwright - nr
Emma L. Cartwright - nr
Mrs. Joseph North Morris- nr
Nimrod Lanphere - nr
Orson Maxson - dis Mar 3, 1892

Debbie Mix - nr
Harriet Wordon - nr
Mrs. Mary Lanphere Terett
Harriet Wilbur Clair
Ester Wells
Clark Wells
Charles Wilbur
George Trask
Rhoda Maxson
H. S. Burdick

CRR 1941.2 Vault
Shinglehouse SDB Church Records 1876-1905
IMS:1995

Bells Run SDB Church 1876-1883
McKean Co PA
Bells Run and Honeoye joined Shinglehouse PA 1883
Five miles NE of Shinglehouse

List of Constituent Members

Nimrod Lanphere
T. W. F. Sage
Edgar Wells
Orson Maxson
Harriet Wilber
Libbie Mix
Esther Wells
Rhoda Maxson

Dea. Clark S. Wells
Alton Maxson
Dea. Charles B. Wilber
Sister Hattie Wells
Sister Sally Lanphere
Sister Harriet Worden
Sister Abigal Sage

Additional Members

Alfonso North
Belle North
Mary Mawfet - ad 1879

Mrs. Charlotte Lamberton - ad 1880
Miss Ada Lamberton

CRR 1941.2 Vault
Bells Run PA Church Records 1876-1882
IMS:1995

Honeoye Branch of Richburg 1870-1883
Located on Honeoye Creek, Potter Co PA
It had 33 members when it and Bells Run joined Shinglehouse
Three miles from Shinglehouse

Members of Record

Dea. Clark Wells,   B. O. Burdick

Letter from B. O. Burdick 1902
Honeoye file - B file
Seventh Day Baptists in Europe and America. Vol II, p. 743
Seventh Day Baptist General Conference 1910

Fox Seventh Day Baptist Church 1827-1834
near Penfield
Clearfield Co. PA
First organized as branch of Berlin NY Church 1818

Members

Dea. John Bliss Sr
John J. Bundy
Job Carr
Stephen Bundy
Francis Goodner
Arnold Bliss
Samuel Ward Bliss
Elisha Weaver
Ranstor Crandall
Reliance B. Bliss
Mary Lucore Bliss (?)
Thomas Bliss (?)
Maria Carr

Reliance Bundy
Ruth Weaver
Justus Kenyon
Justus Kenyon
Freelove Lucore Bliss
Sally Bliss
Lucretia Hewitt
Isaac Bliss
George Bliss
Lydia Doolittle Bliss
Sarah Bundy Bliss
Electa E. Brown Bliss
Jeremiah Bliss

Marriages

Lydia Doolittle - m Isaac Bliss 1831
Arnold Bliss - m Freelove Lucore 1825
George Bliss - m Susan Hunt 1818
John Bliss Jr - b 1792, m Phebe Sherwood, b 1800
Jeremiah Bliss - b 1789, m 1819 Mary Lucore, b 1800
Thomas Bliss - b 1794, m Sally Bundy 1824
Isaac Bliss - b 1797, m 1831 Lydia Doolittle, b CT 1805
George Bliss - b 1799, m Susan Hunt, b 1804

From the notebooks of Charles H. Greene
Seventh Day Baptist Historical So., Janesville WI

Seventh Day Baptists in Europe and America
Seventh Day Baptist General Conference. Vol II, p 750

Shiloh PA SDB Church 1798-c1829
Near Meadville, Crawford Co. PA
No primary records extant

**First members came from Piscataway SDB Church, Piscataway, Middlesex Co. NJ,
then Woodbridgetown, Fayette Co. PA
First organized at James Dunn's home on French Creek**

Members

- James Dunn - liscented to preach by Piscataway NJ, ordained by Rev. Samuel Woodbridge in 1804
- Dea. Owen David s/o Rev. Enoch David from Woodbridgetown, Fayette Co. PA
- Philip Dunn
- David Dunn
- David Dunham
- Jonathan David
- Benjamin Thorp - fr Squan, NJ; located briefly, moved to Lambert's Run WV
- Michael Greenlee - fr Squan NJ
- ___?___ Lewis's family - fr near Baltimore MD, moved to Cussawego PA
- Elizabeth Lewis
- Nancy Lewis w/o Isaac Davis
- Martha Lewis
- George Lewis
- John Lewis
- Nathaniel Lewis
- Eber Lewis
- James Lewis
- Morris Cole
- Dea. Isaac Davis
- Morris Cole, moved to Hayfield PA
- Benjamin Stelle
- A Fitz Randolph family lived near Meadville

**From the Notes of Charles H. Green
Shiloh PA files; PA Files
SDB Historical So., Janesville WI**

Seventh Day Baptists in Europe and America. Vol II, p. 730
Seventh Day Baptist General Conference 1910

Hayfield Seventh Day Baptist Church 1829-c1862
Hayfield Twsp, Crawford Co. (near Saegertown) PA
Meadville Address
Organized from Shiloh PA SDB Church in 1829

Members

Moses Crosley Sr
Richard Crosley
Nathan Crosley
Moses Crosley Jr
Elijah Crosley
Samuel Palmer
Stephen Palmer
Welcome Palmer
Stannet Palmer
Sidney Curtis

Maxson Greenlee
Rylan Greenlee
William Greenlee
John Greenlee
Gilbert Greenlee
Holton Dunn
Simeon Dunn
Louis Dunn
Morris Cole, pastor
Walter Dunn

Hayfield SDB Church History
PA files, B-files
SDB Historical So., Janesville, WI
Seventh Day Baptists in Europe and America Vol II, p. 731
Seventh Day Baptist General Conference 1910

Other Hayfield Members

Eld. Job Tyler
Dea. Lewis A. Dunham, clerk
Dea. David Dunn
Morris Cole, licentiate
Clark Potter, licentiate
Dea. John M. Mills

Dea. Jesse Rowley
Eld. Thomas B. Brown
Rld. Leman Andrus
Eld. Thomas E. Babcock
Dea. Benjamin Stelle
E. Saunders, clerk

Allegany Association SDB Records 1836-1844
MS 19x.214.1
V-E-file

Cussewago SDB Church 1853-c1883
Hayfield Twsp, Crawford Co. PA
No primary records extant
Organized from Shiloh and Hayfield

Known Members

Calvin Waldo
Polly Waldo w/o Calvin
Daniel C. Waldo - arrested for working on Sunday

Claire Waldo w/o Daniel
Lucinda Waldo w/o Daniel

Letter from Mabelle Willmarth, descendent/Waldos,
Saegertown PA

Hickernell SDB Church
Arose out of the ruins of Cussewago, Hayfield and Shiloh 1902-c1910
Seventh Day Baptists in Europe and America. Vol II, p. 731
Seventh Day Baptist General Conference 1910

VI. APPENDIX

Civil War Sabbath-keeping Soldiers
Western NY and Northwest PA

New York Churches
Second Alfred (Alfred Station) SDB Church

John C. Vincent - honorable discharge
Thomas Hull - d of disease
Anthony V. Shaw - d of disease
Harrison W. Green - honorable discharge
Alvin A. Williams - d in Louisiana
Luke Green 2nd - honorable discharge
Andrew J. Allen - honorable discharge
Daniel Green - honorable discharge
Henry Shaw - d
Elberton Potter - honorable discharge
Chauncey Witter - honorable discharge
Nathan Forbes - honorable discharge
Thomas Tefft - hororable discharge
Samuel Whitford - honorable discharge
Nathan H. Vincent - honorable discharge
Slyvester V. Barber - d
Martin Barber - honorable discharge
John Cottrell - honorable discharge
Lester D. Lewis - honorable discharge
Augustus K. Ryno - honorable discharge
Phineas Shaw - honorable discharge
Andrew Satterlee - honorable discharge
Marshal Thomas - honorable discharge
Asher Williams - honorable discharge
Collins Burdick - honorable discharge
Samuel Butler - d
Francello Hull - honorable discharge
Varnum Hull - honorable discharge
Son of Varnum Hull - honorable discharge
Russel Palmiter - d
John Burdick - d
John C. Burdick - honorable discharge
John Morgan - honorable discharge
Frank Maxson - d
Paulding Vincent - d
Samuel A. Wescott - honorable discharge
George Wescott - honorable discharge
Frank Bea - honorable discharge
Ray Millard - honorable discharge
Joseph Cooper - honorable discharge
John Hemphill - honorable discharge

Independence NY Church

Ethan Green - d
L. E. Livermore - honorable discharge
Ira L. Crandall - honorable discharge
Lester Eaton - d
Charles F. Davis - honorable discharge
F. M. Bassett - honorable discharge
Delos Remington - honorable discharge
James R. Crandall - honorable discharge
E. P. Wells - d
Henry Graves - honorable discharge
Daniel Graves - honorable discharge
Mariam Wood - honorable discharge
George A. Green - honorable discharge
Albert Haseltine - d
Orson Kenyon - d
James Livermore - honorable discharge
Oscar F. Burdick - honorable discharge
William H. Clark - d
Orville G. Clark - honorable discharge
Robert Ware - d
Albert Clark - honorable discharge
Jacob Graves - d
Laderna Wood - honorable discharge
Henry Stillman - honorable discharge
Jerome Remington - honorable discharge
Oscar Remington - honorable discharge
Allen Livermore - honorable discharge
Abial Laforge - honorable discharge
Levi Card - d

Hartsville SDB Church

Ephraim C. Truman - honorable discharge
Reuben Potter - d
James Coon - d
John Groves - killed
Orlow Emerson - d
Alonzo Woodard - honorable discharge
Stephen Clark - honorable discharge
Silas Witter - honorable discharge
Slyvanus Whitford - honorable discharge
George Emerson - honorable discharge
Hiram Grow - honorable discharge
Leroy Witter - honorable discharge
Wells Burdick - honorable discharge
Daniel Cornish - honorable discharge
Milo Green - honorable discharge

Scio SDB Church

Lewis C. Burdick - honorable discharge
Ethan M. Stillman - honorable discharge
C. W. Youngs - d
Almon Burdick - d
Charles Freeman - honorable discharge
Lyman Stillman - honorable discharge
George H. Rowley - honorable discharge
William H. Miller - honorable discharge
H. Stell - honorable discharge
C. S. Casteline - honorable discharge
Curtis L. Burdick - d

Friendship (Nile) SDB Church

Warren Allen - honorable discharge
Leander Phillips - d
O. E. Lanphere - d
C. H. Witter - d
G. B. Tanner - d
Julius A. Crandall - d
L. H. Kenyon - honorable discharge
Oscar Kenyon - honorable discharge
J. C. Crandall - honorable discharge
William Wightman - honorable discharge
Samuel Burdick - honorable discharge
Paul B. Clark - honorable discharge
Silas Clark - d
Monroe Strong - honorable discharge
Miriam Strong - honorable discharge
Marshal Allen - honorable discharge
Arthur Allen - honorable discharge
William H. Wells - honorable discharge

Richburg SDB Church

A. B. Cottrell - honorable discharge
E. P. Rogers - honorable discharge
Almond Rogers - honorable discharge
Nathaniel W. Putnam - honorable discharge
W. H. Stillman - honorable discharge
Morris H. Coats - honorable discharge
Schuyler Maxson - d
Cassius Maxson - killed
Addison Evans - honorable discharge
Orrin C. Rogers - honorable discharge
Russel J. Maxson - honorable discharge
Henry D. Lewis - d
John G. Fuller - honorable discharge
Orson Randolph - d
Joseph C. Maxson - honorable discharge
William Champlin - d

Third Genesee (West Genesee) SDB Church

E. W. Irish - honorable discharge
George H. Irish - d
J. M. Crandall - d
Marcus M. Crandall - killed
Floyd M. Crandall - d
Silas G. Burdick - honorable discharge
Lavern Burdick - honorable discharge
George R. Brown - d
Eli P. Brown - d
Andrew N. Brown - d
Lewis Champlin - d
John Champlin - honorable discharge
Marion M. Maxson - d

Second Genesee (Portville) SDB Church

A. D. Hamilton - honorable discharge
C. W. Hamilton - honorable discharge
I. T. Lewis - honorable discharge
S. L. Maxson - honorable discharge
P. Barber - honorable discharge
R. A. Coon - honorable discharge
O. T. Maxson - honorable discharge
J. S. Main - honorable discharge
W. N. Maxson - killed
J. A. Burdick - honorable discharge
M. L. Maxson - honorable discharge
P. V. Maxson - honorable discharge
A. M. Smith - honorable discharge
J. J. Langworthy - honorable discharge
E. N. Crandall - honorable discharge
B. A. Barber - honorable discharge

First Genesee (Little Genesee) SDB Church

Henry C. Rogers - d
Clinton R. Lewis - honorable discharge
Warren W. Jaques - honorable discharge
Sebeus B. Coon - honorable discharge
Delos Barber - honorable discharge
Gurdon W. Lane - d
William B. Bliss - d
Addison A. Burdick - d
George H. Crandall - honorable discharge
John H. Crandall - honorable discharge
William H. Crandall - killed
Henry R. Maxson - honorable discharge
Winfield S. Wells - honorable discharge
Ralph C. Langworthy - honorable discharge
Daniel A. Langworthy - honorable discharge
J. H. Stone - honorable discharge
Albert R. Crandall - honorable discharge
Joel B. Crandall - honorable discharge
Z. P. Maxson - honorable discharge
Dewane D. Babcock - honorable discharge
Henry Coleman - honorable discharge
George L. Utter - honorable discharge
George H. Case - honorable discharge
Orson Lackey - killed
Lafayette Jaques - honorable discharge
Jerry K. Redding - honorable discharge
Arthur J. Hall - honorable discharge
Walter Crandall - honorable discharge
George Whitford - honorable discharge
William W. Stanard - honorable discharge
Morton L. Spencer - honorable discharge
Frederick Spencer - honorable discharge
Israel Spencer - honorable discharge
B. C. Buton - honorable discharge
William A. Jennings - killed
Albino R. Stone - honorable discharge
Olin Langworthy - honorable discharge
Hosea Palmer - d
Edwin Foster - honorable discharge
Morton D. Crandall - honorable discharge
Joseph D. Stillman - honorable discharge
Lyman O. Slade - honorable discharge
Milford D. Hall - honorable discharge
A. D. Green - honorable discharge
Thomas G. Crandall - honorable discharge
Edwin S. Bliss - honorable discharge

Pennsylvania Churches

Hebron SDB Church

S. S. Greenman - honorable discharge
Elno E. Burdick - honorable discharge
Roswell Burton - d
Henry Dingman - honorable discharge
L. H. Hall - honorable discharge
Almeron Burdick - d
Albert Reed - honorable discharge
A. R. Stillman - honorable discharge
William Dingman - honorable discharge
A. H. Ostrander - honorable discharge
C. H. Hydorn - killed
S. R. Green - honorable discharge
Birney Stillman - honorable discharge
Edwin Bickford - d
George E. Green - honorable discharge

Cussewago SDB Church

George Cole - honorable discharge
H. Bolster - killed
Morris Cole - killed
William Hayes - honorable discharge
Mandred Hayes - honorable discharge
John E. Hayes - d

The Sabbath Recorder Vol. XXII, no. 26, p. 102
June 28, 1866
IMS: 1995

Ministers Whom the Churches of the Western Association Have Given to the Seventh Day Baptist Denomination 1810 - 1910

First Alfred:
  Daniel Babcock
  Richard Hull
  Spencer Sweet
  Roy Green
  Nathan V. Hull
  Varnum Hull
  Oliver Perry Hull
  Hamilton Hull
  Jonathan Allen
  P. S. Crandall
  Nathan Wardner
  Oliver D. Sherman
  Judson G. Burdick
  Earl P. Saunders

Second Alfred:
  Stephen Burdick
  Alvin A. Lewis

Friendship:
  Walter B. Gillette
  A. A. F. Randolph
  James L. Scott
  Theodore L. Gardiner

Independence:
  Leander E. Livermore

First Genesee:
  Henry P. Greene
  Paul Burdick

Richburg:
  Rowse Babcock
  Ira Lee Cottrell
  George M. Cottrell

Clarence:
  James H. Cochran
  Thomas R. Williams

Persia:
  Russell G. Burdick
  Oscar Babcock
  George C. Babcock
  Thomas E. Babcock
  Charles P. Rood

Scio:
  A. A. Place

First Hebron:
  William L. Burdick

Willing (formerly Scio)
  Charles Rowley

Portville:
  Sanford L. Maxson

Third Genesee:
  A. G. Crofoot

Pendleton:
  Leman Andrus

Hartsville:
  Hiram P. Burdick
  Hiram Cornwell

Wellsville:
  Henry L. Jones

Foreign Missionaries Who Have Been Selected from the Western Association

First Alfred: Nathan Wardner; Susie M. Burdick
Independence: Olive Forbes Wardner; Lucy Green Randolph
Friendship: Sarah Gardiner Davis

Seventh Day Baptists in Europe and America. Vol II, p. 766-7
Seventh Day Baptist General Conference 1910

List of Churches within Present Bounds of the Western Association

Name	Members at Organization	Maximum Membership	Year of Organization	Year of Closing
Shiloh PA			c 1800	1829
First Alfred	87	602	1816	-------
Friendship (1st)	26	150	1824	c1830
Troupsburg			1824	c1835
Independence (1st)			1824	c1829
Independence (2nd	33		1833	1975
Friendship (2nd Nile)	40	185	1834	1959
Fox			1827	1834
First Genesee (Cuba)	105	219	1827	-----
Richburg (Bolivar, Wirt)	36	135	1827	-----
Clarence (Penbroke- Darien)	62	216	1828	1873
Hayfield	39	72	1829	1862
Second Alfred	191	260	1831	-----
Persia (Perrysburg)	37	75	1832	1858
Hebron	42	102	1834	-----
Scio (Amity)	40	40	1834	1885
Willing (Scio)	27	42	1834	1861
Second Genesee	34	66	1834	1861
Portville	36	67	1834	1862
Third Genesee (1st)	25		1835	1843
3rd Genesee (2nd) (West Genesee)	27	67	1843	1896
Pendleton	19	23	1844	1873
Ulysses	16	16	1845	1862
Hartsville	75	105	1849	c1932
Darien-Cowlesville	33		1851	1873
Cussewago	18	46	1853	1882
Wilson			1855	1862
Honeoye Branch	16		1870	1883
Andover	43	86	1871	1953
Allegheny River			1871	c1877
Hebron Center	34	38	1871	1953
Scio Branch	18		1871	1882
Oswayo PA	28		1871	1880
Clarence & Pendleton	13		1875	1883
Stannards' Corners	12		1875	1880
Bells Run	15		1876	1883
Hornellsville	25	48	1877	1914
Elmira NY	4		1883	1888
Shinglehouse	41	41	1883	1920
Wellsville	17	47	1885	1911
Hickernell	18		1902	1910

***Seventh Day Baptists In Europe and America.* Vol II, p. 748**
Seventh Day Baptist General Confrence 1910
Updated IMS: 1995

WESTERN NEW YORK STATE AND NORTHWESTERN PENNSYLVANIA

Showing conties and approximate location
of Seventh Day Baptist Churches
(See next page for inset map of
Allegany and Potter Counties)

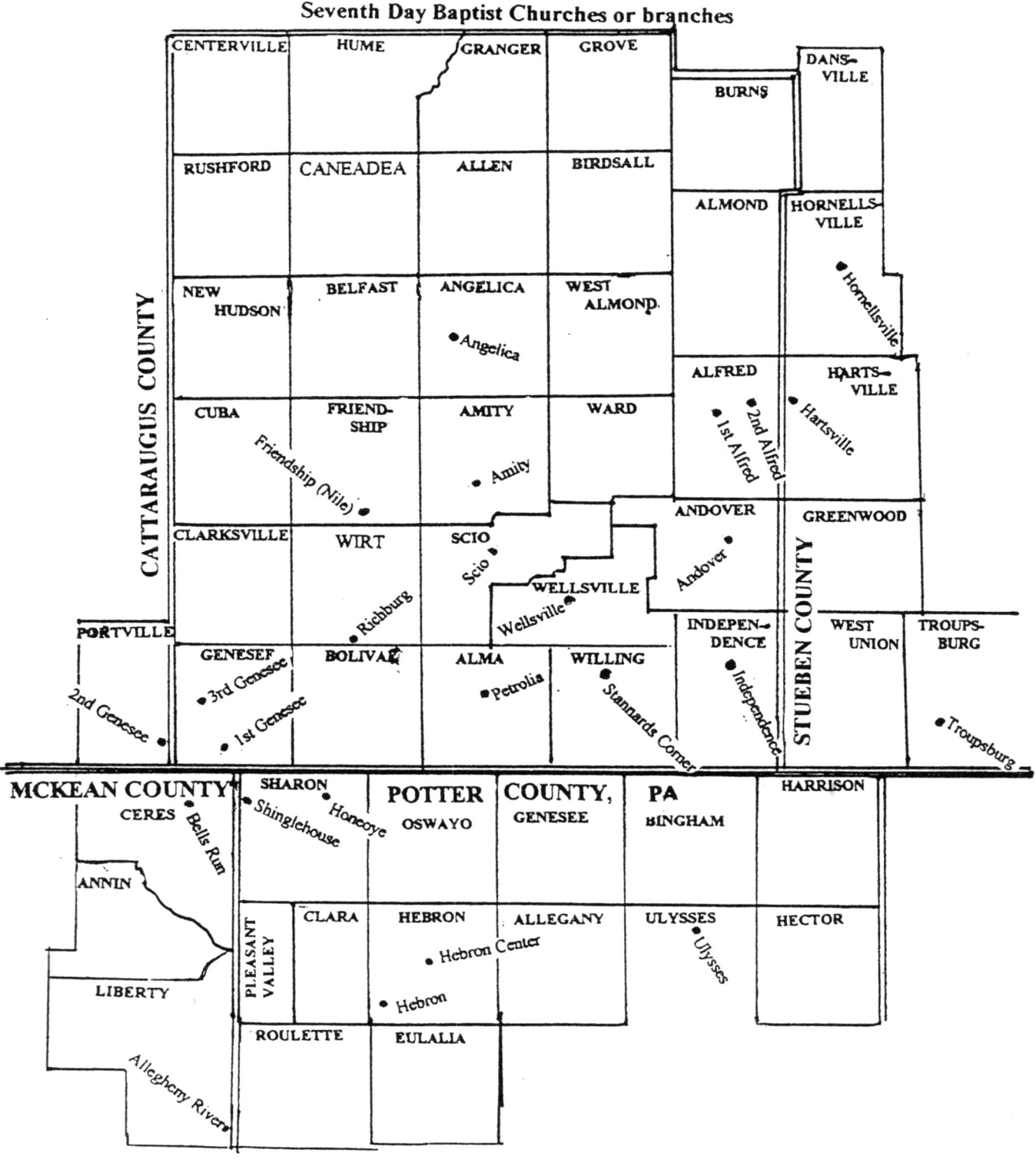

SURNAME INDEX

Ackley, 79
Alcott, 73
Allen, 5-8 15 16 32-39 41-43 45 49 51 95 96 99
Almy, 32
Alott, 36
Amadown, 31
Andrus, 39 46 47 74 75 94 99
Antisdale, 66 67
Atkins, 80 85
Atkinson, 85 86
Austin, 12 72 73 76
Ayars-Ayres, 28 35-38 41 45 58 60 63 73 80 83-85
Aylesworth, 73
Babcock, 1-4 7 9 10 16 22 23 25 38-43 45-48 53-57 59 60 68 74 77 79 80-82 94 97 99
Backus, 20 22 32 33 52 60
Bailey, 11 56
Baird, 11
Baker, 3 19 21 25 49 63 64 73 85 86
Bakker, 16
Baldwin, 74
Ball, 86 89
Ballard, 46 48 50 51
Barber, 9 11 12 32 33 54-57 62 65 87 95 97
Bardeen, 15 16 52
Barrett, 76
Bassett, 23-26 52 79 95
Baxter, 57 61
Bea, 95
Bebee, 1 2
Becker, 15 28
Beckworth, 10
Beebe, 3 7 9 12 13 18-20
Beeman, 78
Bell, 59
Below, 73
Beman, 73
Benchoff, 90
Benjamin, 1 3 4 6 8 12 23 25 31
Bennehoff, 59
Bennett, 11 24 27

Benny, 3
Bentley, 1 4 9 10
Berkhardt, 83
Berry, 59
Beverly, 80
Beyea, 12
Beyece, 11
Bickford, 98
Billiard, 73
Birmingham, 28
Blake, 4
Blakely, 79 80
Blanchard, 76
Bland, 57
Bliss, 47-51 53-59 68 92 97
Bliven, 1 29-31 45 62
Bloomer, 1 3
Bloss, 26
Bly, 89
Bolster, 98
Boone, 68
Booth, 89
Boss, 53 56-58
Bowen, 75 78
Bowers, 20
Bowler, 55 58 68
Bozzard, 19
Bradford, 90
Brafford, 52
Bridge, 90
Bristol, 60 61
Brock, 81-86
Brooks, 1
Brosheion, 51
Brown, 19 23-25 37 38 43 45 52 56 57 63-66 77 79 80 94 96
Bryant, 15
Bullock, 52 56 59
Bundy, 92
Burdick, 1-16 18-20 22-26 28 30 32 37-44 47 49 51-62 65 66 68 72 73 75-80 83-88 90 91 95-99
Burton, 82 84 98
Bush, 80

Butler, 7 72 95
Buton, 54 55 57 97
Butterfield, 11
Buyer, 25
Camp, 80
Campbell, 37 45 46 55 65 79
Canfield, 31
Card, 23-25 27 95
Carl, 74
Carpenter, 56-59 72 87
Carr, 11 92
Carter, 48
Cartwright, 8 11 19 29-31 43 46-52 55 90 91
Case, 46-48 50 57 58 97
Cass, 43 44
Casteline, 90 96
Chamberlin, 89
Champlin, 41 46-51 54 55 60 63-66 96
Chapman, 25
Chase, 15
Cheesebrough, 1-3 5 73
Childs, 38 63 66
Clair, 8 19 89 91
Clark, 11 14 15 23-26 29 34 36 38 42 43 59-61 72 73 76 95 96
Clarke, 18-22 25 37-44 60 61 72 76
Clawson, 54
Cleare, 5
Cleaveland, 46
Clemens, 90
Coats, 36-38 44 46-51 96
Coburn, 74
Cochran, 4 6 16 72 99
Cole, 5 7 36 62 93 94 98
Colegrove, 9 11 68
Coleman, 97
Colgrove, 58
Coller, 32 40-42
Collins, 8 11 19 49 58 60 87
Combs, 86
Compton, 39 41
Connor, 61

Conover, 11
Conser, 60
Converse, 5
Cook, 5 6 8 10 12 13 18 72
Coon, 1-4 7 8 14 21 22 24 29 30
    36-38 41-43 46 53-60 62-66
    68 72 73 81 96 97
Cooper, 59 68 95
Corbon, 56
Cornice, 15
Cornish, 11 96
Cornwell, 14 16 56 99
Cotten, 36 37 41
Cottrell, 7 10 12 16 22 23 28 34
    46-52 69 72 73 80 95 96 99
Covey, 35 36 43 50 52
Crandal, 18
Crandall, 9 10 14 16 22-26 32
    33 35-43 45-49 51-60 62-69
    72 75 79 80 92 96 97 99
Cranson, 64
Crocker, 89
Crofoot, 22 33 39 66 99
Crosley, 94
Culver, 38
Cummings, 58 66 69 78
Curtis, 16 38 40 42 75 94
Dacon, 36
Dana, 58 60
Daniels, 42-44 46 48-51
David, 93
Davidson, 32 33 35 41-44 50 51
Davis, 1 2 4 6 7-9 11 14-16 18
    22-25 28 29 31 32 35 37 39
    49 51 75-77 82 90 93 95 99
Davy, 55
Day, 37 46 73
Dean, 82 88
Degrater, 89
Degroff, 59
Delong, 52
Deming, 4 6 7 13 23
Deo, 56
Dibble, 89
Dickerson, 69
Dingman, 82 84-87 98
Dixson, 73
Doolittle, 92
Downey, 78
Downs, 14
Drake, 2 54
Dunham, 35 93 94
Dunn, 35 93 94
Dutcher, 39
Dye, 43 46-48 50 72
Eastman, 5 6 8

Eaton, 23-25 41 54 95
Eddy, 47 79 80
Edmonds, 59
Edwards, 11 12 40 42 54-57
Eggleston, 18
Ehret, 18
Eldred, 73
Eldridge, 39
Elliot, 6
Elliott, 4 7 32 58
Ellis, 2 3 4 7
Elster, 32
Elston, 33
Emerson, 3 4 5 8 10 11 15 34
    51 85 86 89 96
Emery, 5
Ennis, 53 54 58
Enos, 38 43
Ensworth, 58
Esklemon, 43
Evans, 2 43 45-47 83 84 88 96
Everett, 18
Fairbanks, 57-60 63 69
Fairchild, 59
Farley, 59 60
Farnam, 75
Fenner, 10 11
Ferrand, 84
Ferris, 11
Ferron, 82
Finch, 73
Firington, 64
Fish, 6 24 31
Fisk, 12 16 25 27 28 37 52
Fitz,
Fleming, 39 41
Flint, 31
Forbes, 8 10 15 24 28 95
Foster, 45 48-51 57 58 97
Fox, 57
Frank, 12 15 16
Franklin, 1 14
Freeman, 58 96
Fries, 43
Fugan, 58
Fuller, 12 40 42 44-48 50 52
    72-74 96
Fullmer, 74 75 78
Gale, 59 89
Gardiner, 11 18 37-43 63 64 66
    69 79 99
Gavit, 4
Gear, 43
George, 49
German, 39 42 98
Gibbs, 59 60 69 82-85 88

Giddings, 37 38
Gilbert, 15 45 46-50 57
Gillette, 35 40 42 46 47 99
Gillings, 78
Glover, 25 49
Goff, 16
Goodliff, 32 33
Goodner, 92
Goodrich, 29
Goodwin, 80 89
Graves, 24 25 95
Green, 1-13 18-20 22 23 25 26
    28 30 32 33 35-39 41-43 46
    49 51 53-58 60 61 63-66 69
    72 76 80 82-85 95-99
Greene, 16 18 22 30 31 37 69
    99
Greenlee, 93 94
Greenman, 3 5 6 42 72 73 76 77
    79 81 84 86 89 98
Gridley, 11
Griffin, 47 48 50 52
Grinnell, 7
Grinwald, 4
Griswold, 22-24 55
Groves, 86 96
Grow, 15 16 61 96
Gruman, 35-37
Hadley, 11 12
Hadsall, 5
Hadsell, 8 11
Hall, 4 6-8 11 13 15 20 21 24
    55-57 59 60 69 82 84 97 98
Hallock, 32 33 82-84 88
Hally, 82
Hamilton, 3 4 6 8 9 11 22 24 39
    41 43 46 97
Hammond, 80
Hand, 37
Hannan, 11
Hardy, 5 10
Harmon, 10
Harris, 11 29 76 82 88 89
Harry, 22
Harvey, 51 72
Haseltine, 23 95
Hassard, 39
Hatas, 2
Hatch, 74 75
Hawkins, 79 80
Hawkl, 2
Hawley, 39 83 84
Hayes, 98
Hazard, 60
Hazeltine, 25
Head, 1-3 51

Heges, 81
Helton, 74
Hemphill, 7 9 11 89 95
Hendrix, 58
Herrington, 8
Hewitt, 92
Hill, 1-3 25 76 77
Hiscock, 60
Hitchcock, 80
Hoag, 76
Hockins, 79
Hodgkess, 74
Hodgkins, 75
Hofer, 20
Hoffman, 12
Hoford, 49
Holbridge, 72
Holcomb, 36
Holtin, 36
Hood, 14-16 28 49-52
Hopkins, 49 51
Hornblower, 55 69
Hotchkiss, 32 33
Howard, 66 76 77
Howe, 31 59 90
Howel, 4
Hubbard, 37-39 41
Hubble, 43
Hudson, 36
Huff, 36
Huffman, 39
Hulbert, 69
Hulett, 58-60
Hull, 1-5 7-10 16 31 35 49 60 72 73 79-81 95 99
Humphrey, 4
Hunt, 10 73 74 76 78 92
Hunting, 47
Hurd, 37
Hutchens, 16
Hutchinson, 59
Hyde, 38 40-42 54 63 64
Hydorn, 81-84 98
Hyett, 36
Irish, 9 20 32 33 39 41 42 44 47 48 63-66 69 96
Jacobs, 25 38 39 47
Jacques-Jaques, 8 56-60 69 97
Jennings, 97
Jennison, 58
Johnson, 35-39 41 42 84 88
Jones, 4 6 8 32 33 72 99
Jordan, 16 34 40 42 43 50 51 57 59
Joy, 58
Kalley, 16

Karr, 12
Keller, 14 15 52 65-67
Kellogg, 79
Kelly, 28 43
Kelsey, 23 25
Kenny, 78
Kenyon, 4 5 7 8 10 17 18 22-24 34-36 38 41 42 46-50 53 55 57-60 66 67 85 86 89 90 92 95 96
Kettle, 15
King, 17 48-52
Knickerbocker, 87 89
Knox, 24 25 32 33
Lackey, 53-57 59 62 97
Lafarge, 95
Lamb, 87
Lamberton, 86 91
Lamm, 66
Lane, 56 97
Langdon, 24
Langworthy, 4-13 18-20 53-59 70 73 97
Lanphere, 1-5 7-9 13 18 19 37 38 43 46 49 52 56 59 60 90 91 96
Lasher, 24 25 32 43
Latham, 42 43
Lathrop, 39
Lawrence, 87
Lebar, 46
Lee, 25
Lenox, 36
Leonard, 15
Leskin, 1
Lester, 30
Levins, 23 23
Lewis, 2-12 15 18 24 34 43 46 49 56-60 66 67 70 74 82 89 93 95-97 99
Lioms, 60
Livermore, 11 18 19 22-25 65 95 99
Longmate, 74 75 78
Loomer, 79
Loomis, 58
Loring, 32 33
Loveland, 39 41
Lovell, 85
Luce, 81-86
Lucore, 92
Lusk, 12 20
Luther, 36
Lyman, 72 88
Lynch, 5 8 82
Lyons, 52

Maase, 46
Main, 12 28 62 65 81 82 97
Manning, 9
Manroe, 4 5 7 9-12 50 51 60
Marian, 32
Marrow, 2
Marsh, 90
Martin, 51
Marvin, 50
Maryiot-Marriat, 23 46
Maryiot-Marriot, 53 54 55 56
Matteson, 84-87 89
Mattison, 15
Mawfet, 91
Maxson, 1 3-7 9 12 17 18 22 28 30 31 35-39 41 45-59 62-66 70 76 77 90 91 95-97 99
Mccaleb, 73
Mccarn, 24
Mccoon, 82
Mccray, 15
Mcdougal, 14 15
Mcgibeny, 48
Mcgibney, 46 50
McHenry, 11
Mchenry, 12
Mckee, 43 89
Mckelvey, 70
Mckune, 25
Mclaferday, 36
Mead, 75
Menney, 14
Merkt, 11 9
Merrit, 17 54 70
Merritt, 22 50 51
Messenger, 35 45 48-51
Messinger, 46 47
Metz, 50
Millard, 3 30 59 85 86 95
Miller, 32 33 41 50 51 96
Mills, 32-36 94
Miner, 3
Mistoe, 33
Mitchell, 86
Mix, 39 41-43 49 52 90 91
Moland, 20
Monson, 89
Moore, 73
Moose, 46
Morehouse, 90
Morgan, 25 73 78 95
Morris, 38 90 91
Morrison, 48
Morton, 36
Moses, 51
Mosher, 18 31 48

Mowatt, 83
Munger, 66
Murry, 64
Nelson, 89
Neph, 14
Nichols, 8 6 9
Noble, 35 73
Noise, 63 64
Norris, 55
North, 90 91
Noyce, 65
Nye, 54 63 64
Ockerman, 31
Odell, 11
Oliver, 65 66
Ormsby, 11 12 9
Ostrander, 83-86 98
Oviatt, 30
Pace, 39
Page, 24 25 27
Palmer, 12 28 48 52 54 62 82 88 90 94 97
Palmiter, 1 3 4 7 9-12 14 15 95
Parcell, 36
Parker, 25
Paxton, 24
Payne, 64 65
Pease, 11 80
Peckham, 39
Perkins, 23 32 43 49 51 59 86
Perry, 2 3 10 11 20 21 37 59 61
Peters, 79 80
Petitt, 58 59 60
Pettibone, 8 14-17 28
Phelps, 6 14
Phillips, 34 35 46 48 96
Pierce, 45 79
Pitts, 48
Place, 3 5 7-9 31 38 39 41 86 99
Platts, 18 28 39
Polan, 17
Pope, 15 16
Popple, 2
Post, 74
Potter, 1 2 4 6 8 9 10-12 14-17 20 21 23-25 37 38 46 53-55 65 70 72 74 94-96
Powell, 60
Pratt, 4 72
Prentice, 79 80
Preston, 60
Price, 64
Prince, 66
Prindle, 57 58
Pringle, 56
Prosser, 57 59 64 65

Putman, 49
Putnam, 96
Randall, 79 80 82-87
Randolph, 22 32 33 35 36 46-48 50 51 53 93 96 99
Reading, 23-25
Redding, 97
Redfield, 21
Redner, 73 89
Reed, 46-50 58 63 82-84 86 98
Reeland, 61
Remington, 21-23 25 50 95
Reynolds, 23 25 59 81-84 86 87
Rhedfield, 80
Richardson, 72
Riddle, 52
Rightingbark, 46
Roan, 28
Robbins, 38
Roberts, 12 31
Robertson, 42
Robinson, 58 77 90
Rogers, 10 17 29 30 31 36 37 39-43 45 46 48-52 54-56 70 96 97
Rood, 73 80 99
Root, 10 45 55
Rose, 12 52
Rosebloom, 89
Rosebush, 23-25
Ross, 70
Rowley, 31 32 94 96 99
Roxy, 17
Rudiger, 10 9
Russell, 73
Ryno, 36 37 46 48-51 95
Sackey, 57
Saddler, 43
Sage, 31 90 91
Sampson, 88
Sanden, 80
Sanders, 3
Sanford, 18 22 26 58-61 64-66 70
Santee, 28
Satterlee, 1-3 7 9 14 46 48 50-52 54 80 95
Saunders, 1 3-9 10 38 45 47-49 51 52 54-56 60 63-65 72 76 77 80 94 99
Scott, 37 45 46 48 70 99
Serbner, 80
Severance, 18
Severson, 59
Sharman, 77
Shaw, 2 4-12 17 28 43 48 89 95

Shay, 82
Sheldon, 54 72 76
Shepherd, 10
Sheppard, 17
Sheriff, 10 11
Sherman, 10 51 75 99
Sherwood, 89 92
Shopbelt, 28
Silk, 73
Simpson, 17
Sinnette, 42 43
Sisson, 38 40-42 63 64 70
Skinner, 43 48 50
Slade, 41 57-60 88 97
Slike, 59
Slingerland, 23 24
Smalley, 35-37
Smith, 1 2 4 6-8 11 17 31 32 34 40 42 44 46 48 49 51-54 60 62-66 72 73 80 88 90 97
Snow, 34 75
Snyder, 12 20 86
Socker, 25
Socwell, 18 21
Sole, 24
Sparks, 81 82
Spencer, 59 97
Spicer, 37-39
Springer, 64
Stannard, 32 35 36 38 41 55 56 71 97
Stanton, 42
Stebbins, 47 49 51 60 61 76 77
Steely, 31
Stelle, 32 93 94 96
Sterns, 3
Stetson, 56
Steven, 60
Stevens, 61
Stewart, 23 24 45 55 79
Stillman, 2 3 5 7 9 10 12 17 22-25 28-33 37 42 43 46-50 52-58 62 71 81-85 89 95-98
Stone, 14 59 97
Stout, 58
Straight, 31
Striker, 31
Strong, 37 39 41 96
Stuck, 36
Sullivan, 21 32 52
Summerbell, 12 43 49 51
Sutherland, 82
Sutton, 18
Swaim, 28
Sward, 3
Swartout, 86

Sweet, 5-9 55
Swift, 9 89
Swinney, 10 11
Symons, 77
Syndal, 17
Tanner, 22 31 38-41 53-57 71 96
Taylor, 3 47 77
Tefft, 3 9-11 95
Terett, 91
Terrell, 10
Tew, 53
Thayer, 11 12 58
Thibbe, 81 82 88
Thogens, 35
Thomas, 12 73 95
Thompson, 15
Thorngate, 73 79 80
Thorp, 93
Threlkeld, 43
Thurston, 37
Tierman, 58
Tinker, 43
Tomkins, 17
Tracy, 86
Trapp, 46
Trask, 50 90 91
Truman, 14 17 37 38 46 64 96
Turner, 12 20 21
Twist, 45
Tyler, 94
Utter, 38 97
Vanhorn, 18
Vandaventer, 74
Vanselor, 37
Vars, 37-39
Vincent, 2 4 7 9-12 40 42 50 51

Vincent (continued) 55 64 65 80 95
Voohees, 24
Voorhees, 25 90 91
Wakely, 58
Walbridge, 80
Waldo, 94
Walker, 12
Walter, 4
Walton, 66 67
Wamsley, 20
Ward, 55 74
Wardner, 9 12 43 58 99
Ware, 19 95
Warner, 90
Warren, 3
Wattenpaugh, 79 80
Weatherby, 37
Weaver, 92
Webb, 4
Webster, 18
Weed, 29 30
Welch, 89
Wells, 10 11 23-26 37 41-43 49 53-57 59 71 74 81 82 85 90 91 95-97
Wescot, 4 7
Wescott, 8 95
West, 4 5 32 38
Weyman, 58
Wheaton, 21
Wheeler, 33 36 37 39 41 83 84
Wheelock, 45
Whitcomb, 12
White, 4 22 42 43 49 51 57 61 82 89
Whitford, 1 3-5 7-12 15-17 42 43 52 79 80 95-97

Wigden, 35 36
Wightman, 38 41 96
Wilber, 3-5 7 10 15 28 59 60 65 66 90 91
Wilcox, 17 28 36 38 43 46 48-51 57
Willard, 35 40-43 58-60
Williams, 5 7-9 18 20 24 25 28 34 36 45 47-49 50 72 73 76 77 85 95 99
Willmarth, 94
Wilson, 71
Winson, 89
Winters, 75
Withy, 1 2
Witt, 75
Witter, 3 4 6-9 10 12 14 15 17 18 20 21 31-34 37-39 40-43 52 57-59 67 95 96
Wood, 6 8 23-25 95
Woodin, 59
Woodruff, 11 9
Woodward, 15 17 28 47 50 51 96
Woolever, 6 8
Woolhizer, 61
Worden, 59
Wordon, 67 71 91
Woren, 90
Wright, 1 11 39 41
Wrightman, 39
Yapp, 35 36 38 63 64 66
Yarrington, 48
York, 3 32-34
Young, 1 4 24 31 64 65 66 96
Zeliff, 9

www.ingramcontent.com/pod-product-compliance
Lightning Source LLC
Chambersburg PA
CBHW081135170426
43197CB00017B/2867